THE LION-DOG
OF BUDDHIST ASIA

THE LION-DOG
OF BUDDHIST ASIA

Elsie P. Mitchell

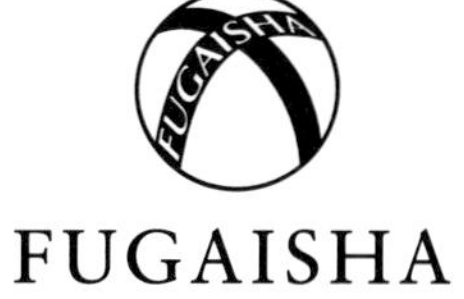

FUGAISHA

Fugaisha books are distributed in the United States
and Canada by Charles E. Tuttle Company, Inc.,
28 South Main Street, Rutland, Vermont 05702-0410.

This book is printed on acid-free paper.

First edition, 1991
Published by Fugaisha, 230 Park Avenue, New York, NY 10017,
with editorial offices in Renens, Switzerland
(Case Postale 411, 1020 Renens, VD 1, Switzerland).
Copyright © 1991 by Elsie P. Mitchell;
all rights reserved. Printed in Japan.

ISBN 0-9628495-0-2 (hardcover)   ISBN 0-9628495-1-0 (paperback)
LCC Card No. 91-70174

To
*John
and to
Cecily and Elspeth,
three good friends of the
dogs of Fo*

CONTENTS

ACKNOWLEDGMENTS

I am exceedingly grateful to many people for their help with this book, as well as for their encouragement.

My husband devoted many hours of help with the manuscript. Elizabeth ten Grotenhuis Flemings made valuable suggestions, particularly for the Japanese chapter. My brother, Edward C. Johnson 3rd, contributed several splendid illustrations. Peter Fetchko of the Peabody Museum of Salem was generous with time and help. Wu Tung showed me many of the stored treasures of the Museum of Fine Arts, Boston, and pointed out dog-lion exhibits I might otherwise have missed. Lei Kai's translations from Chinese and transliteration of Chinese names into pinyin were an important contribution to this book. Lama Khenpo Palden Sherab, Lama Tulku Thondup, and Harold Talbott contributed to my knowledge of the *kang seng* of Tibet. Jack Kimball unearthed some very useful materials for the Tibetan chapter.

Catherine Froeb gave me permission to use the photograph of a courtyard at the château of Fontainebleau, France, taken by the late John R. Hill. Becky Davis and Suzanne Trumbull applied their considerable talents to the design and editing of the lion-dog's story. The photograph on the front of the jacket of the hardcover edition of this book (the front cover of the paperback edition) is by Stephen B. Leek; the photograph on the back of the jacket of the hardcover edition (the back cover of the paperback edition) is by Richard Cheek.

CELESTIAL DOGS, DOG-LIONS, AND LION-DOGS

In the sixth century B.C. in China, fierce demonic dogs were believed to inhabit the far reaches of the heavens as well as the vivid imagination of the Chinese people. One of these celestial dogs, "the monster that howls in the sky," was thought to resemble a shooting star, and his meteorlike appearances were often accompanied by a great deal of noise and light. To prevent this creature from devouring the sun or the moon during an eclipse, the populace, with drums, gongs, and incense, created a general din and much smoke, all of which activity was supposed to frighten away malevolent spirits. Another dog who was thought to live among the stars was a bellicose monster the size of an elephant. A powerful giant with a thick neck and bulging owllike eyes, he entertained himself by snatching children from their families.

By the fifth or sixth century A.D., Buddhism had permeated the fabric of Chinese society to such a degree that even the owl-eyed celestial dog-monster fell under its benevolent spell. His descent from the heavens must have resulted in encounters with an Indian lion, pacified and converted by the Buddha to his Dharma, or doctrine. The fusion of Indian lion and Chinese dog accompanied the Enlightened One's teaching throughout Asia. Replicas of this dog-lion and his mate took up residence at the entrances of Chinese Buddhist temples as well as other buildings of importance. Hereafter, the symbolic guardian creature will be called a dog-lion; his small flesh-and-blood counterpart will be referred to as a lion-dog.

The Chinese rendered the Fu dog, Fo dog, or dog of Fo (dog of Buddha) in ceramics, in bronze, in marble, in serpentine, in chalcedony, and in jade. The Japanese allowed his spirit to express itself in wood, the material which one scholar believes best expresses "le génie de la race." In the ornamental toggles known as *netsuke* the dog-lion, whom the Japanese call the *shishi* or the *kara-shishi* (Chinese dog-lion), sheds his Chinese dignity as he

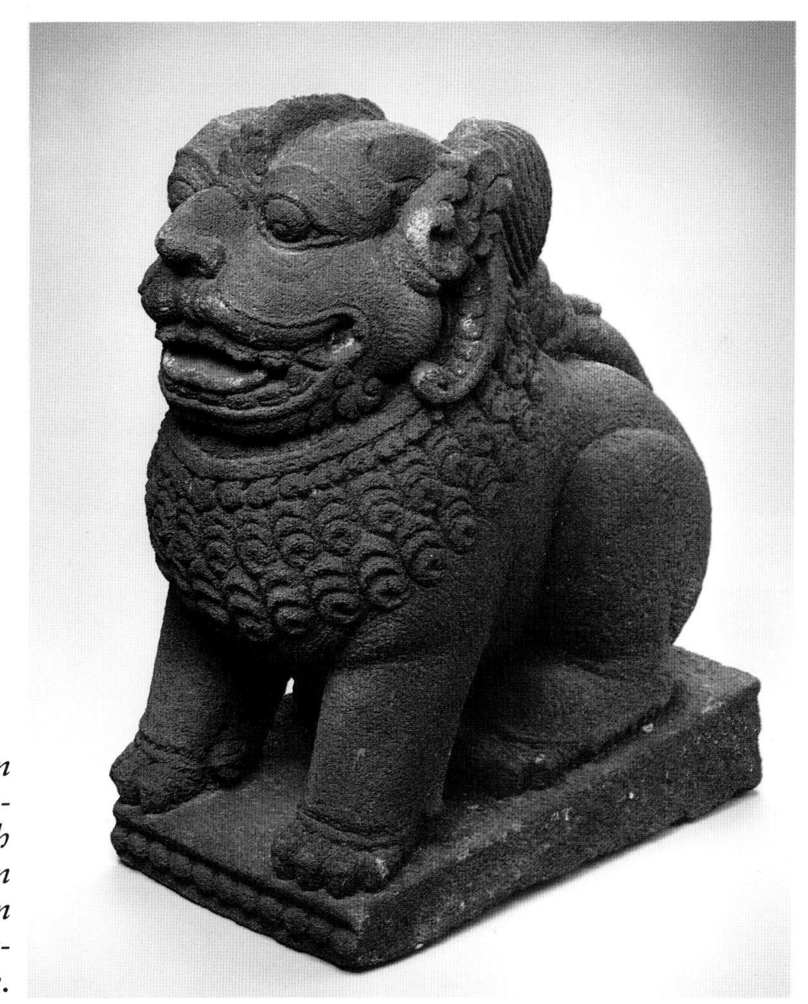

1. *A fierce stone dog-lion from the Lara-Jonggrang temple, Central Java; late ninth or early tenth century* A.D. *Courtesy, Museum of Fine Arts, Boston; gift of John Goelet, Constance B. and Carroll L. Cartwright. By exchange.*

plays with a ball or flower, scratches himself, or wrestles with other shishi. The Buddhist dog-lion/lion-dog is an exuberant breed, both in art and in flesh and fur. His gargoylelike smile, which so beguiles his human friends, may also be found woven or embroidered into fine silk brocades as well as into woolen Chinese and Tibetan carpets.

In the chapters which follow, I shall attempt to present a few highlights of the dog-lion's career as he appeared in myriad art forms in China, Japan, and Tibet. Flesh-and-blood lion-dogs were bred in China and Japan to achieve a likeness to artists' conceptions of the legendary dog-lion, and conversely, artists were influenced by the lion-dogs seen at court and in monasteries. The ancestors of the small, shaggy dogs who shared tent, court, and monastic life with nomads, emperors, and monks will also be introduced in these pages.

A book professing to examine the Buddha's dog-lion would be incomplete without some scrutiny of the place of non-human beings in Buddhist teachings. Chapter six will explore the relationship of non-Buddhist religions, Buddhism, and non-humans.

Some of the religions of antiquity taught benevolence to certain animals. Buddhism and Jainism were distinguished by their teachings of compassion for all creation. The art of Buddhism, its symbols, and its icons were not created as ends in themselves.

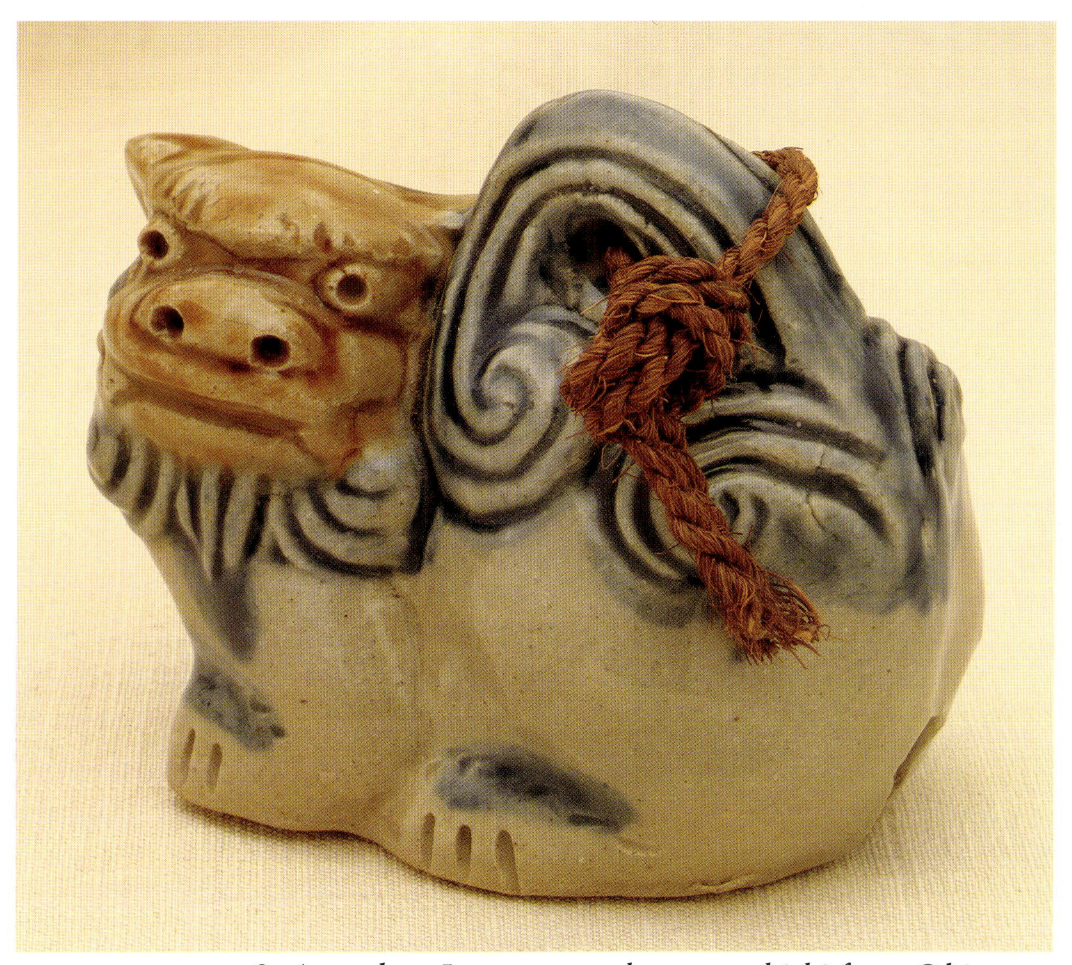

2. *A modern Japanese earthenware shishi from Okinawa.*

They were expected to inspire people to live together, as well as with all other beings, in the spirit of compassion and peace.

Perhaps my reader is wondering about the inspiration for this book, a book which may appear to contain a rather odd agglutination of subjects: legends, some non-human beings, art, and religion. These ingredients fit together very comfortably in a Buddhist context. However, it was an experience in my personal life, a serendipitous visit to France more than forty years ago, which brought together the elements of the book and inspired the research into the subjects found in these pages.

In 1947, I was a few years out of school and on my honeymoon in Paris. Parisians were war weary. There were weevils in the *petits pains,* and in the elegant apartment of my host and hostess the silk carpets, curtains, and cushions were threadbare. Austerities were the order of the day for both the poor and the well-to-do. For many older people who had survived the vicissitudes of the war, it was a contemplative time, a time for much thought and philosophic conversation.

An intense appreciation of whatever, as well as whoever, had been blessed with survival prevailed. This could be an image of fine jade or amber, or a patient and loyal small lion-dog who spent long, uneventful days on a cushion by a drawing room window. My hostess's treasured lion-dog subsisted on an unca-

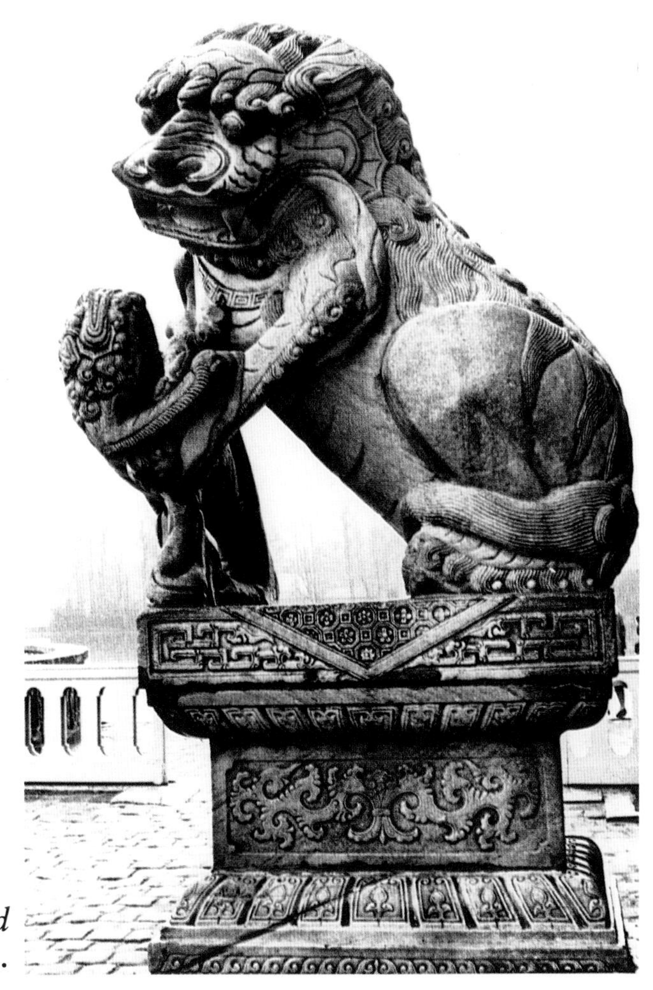

3. *A Chinese stone mother dog-lion and offspring at the château of Fontainebleau.*

nine, if quite Buddhist, diet of vegetable soup, stale bread, potatoes, fruit, an occasional egg, and a little milk. Outside the black market, there was little meat for man or dog.

The dog was called Sing Tow, "lion" in the Thai language. He was the size of a small present-day Shih Tzu, and except for the way the hair grew, or rather did not grow, on his face, he looked like a Shih Tzu. A few of these little dogs were bred in Europe before and during World War II. During the war years the then-rare breed was sometimes kept alive by being interbred with Pekingese. One English breeder collected the wool found in brushes after grooming her Shih Tzu. The wool she had made into yarn, and this was used for knitting articles which were sold in aid of the Red Cross.

Sing Tow's mistress told us that the Portuguese couple from whom she had purchased Sing Tow called him a lion-dog, and by that she supposed they meant he was a Pekingese. They had told her he was rare and special, and had been very distressed to have to part with him.

The owner of Sing Tow was German, the daughter of a Prussian general, and the wife of a man of French-Scottish parentage. The couple resided with Sing Tow in a beautiful apartment in the rue de Lille, in Paris. Their elegant drawing room housed a remarkable collection of Oriental figures of jade, lapis lazuli, am-

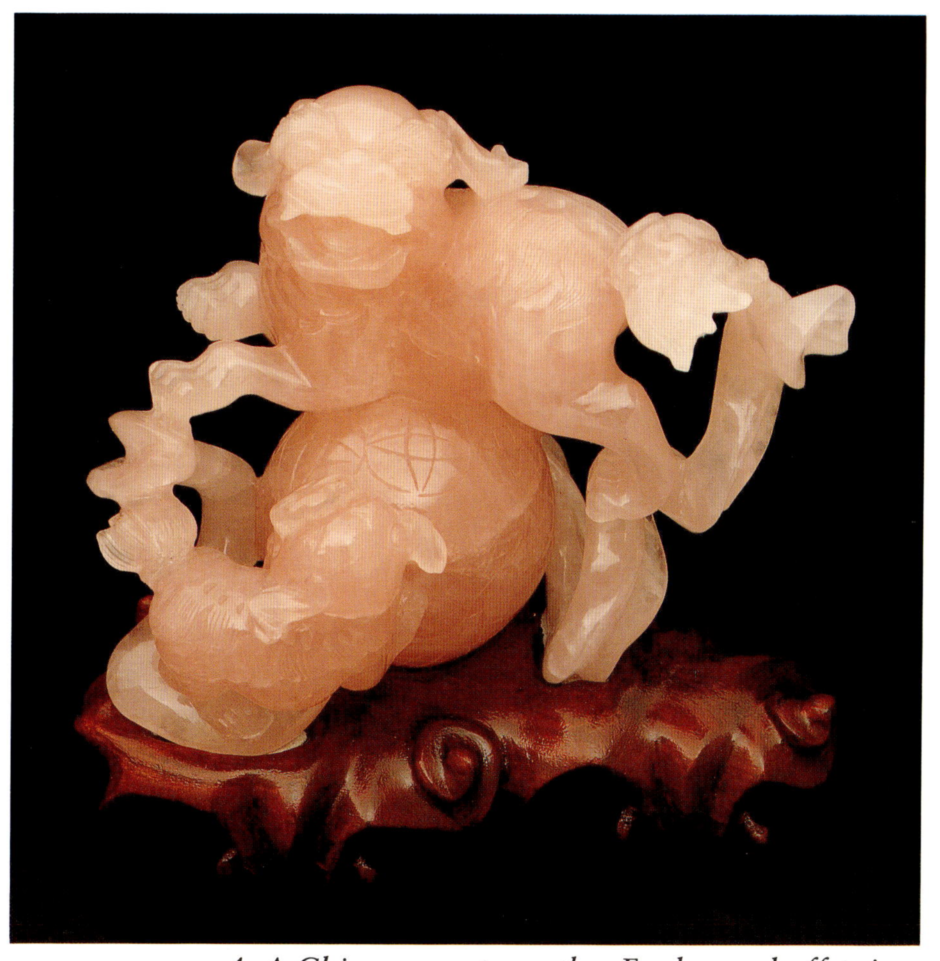

4. A Chinese quartz mother Fu dog and offspring.

ber, and other semiprecious stones, all displayed in specially designed and lighted cabinets.

Sing Tow was acquired by his mistress after her traumatic incarceration in a Paris jail. There she was the "guest," as she wryly put it, of her former countrymen. Her pacifist and anti-Nazi sentiments did not please her jailers; nor did the fact that the lady refused to disclose the location of her husband, who was associated with the Free French in exile. Sing Tow, from the moment he was acquired by his rather formidable mistress, followed her everywhere. He never wore a leash, but on crowded sidewalks and traffic-filled streets he was always at her side.

After the lady's release from prison and her reunion with her husband, the couple, together with Sing Tow, spent part of their time in a converted antique mill in Septeuil, a suburb of Paris. Here Sing Tow appointed himself the guardian of a large flock of ducks, whom he herded about the property. At precisely the same time each day, the ducks were gently but firmly rounded up and shepherded through the French doors and across the stone-tiled floor of the dining room for his mistress's and visitors' inspection. At a word from Madame, the ducks were duly escorted back out into the garden. According to Sing Tow's mistress, this undertaking was wholly her lion-dog's own idea, and was carried out each day they were in residence at the mill.

Sing Tow took his responsibility for his ducks seriously. When I met him in 1947, he had only one eye. The other had been lost about a year earlier in the course of an altercation with a German Shepherd from a neighboring property, the Shepherd having attempted to make off with one of Sing Tow's charges.

Sing Tow, maintaining admirable Buddhist equanimity, was frequently chauffeured around Paris, through the French countryside, and occasionally into Italy or Portugal in a large old Citroën, a car favored by gangsters in French movies of the 1940s. Sing Tow's master and mistress, both very portly people weighing close to two hundred pounds, were ballast for the front of the car. The rear seat, separated from the front seat by more than three feet, fishtailed wildly around corners as the driver (either Monsieur or Madame) piloted the vehicle at top speed through the countryside, horn blaring and tires squealing. Human occupants of that back seat were often reduced to catatonic jelly as they were hurtled through the narrow streets of small villages and around sharp bends. Seated on the slippery leather seat, Sing Tow bore himself with leonine patience and dignity.

He was equally at home in the elegant drawing room above the rue de Lille, with its museumlike display of Oriental treasures. Many of these rare and interesting pieces, which included assorted creatures of mythology, had been presented to Sing

Tow's master by the king of Siam, for whom he had been the purchasing agent. The drawing room was entered through a large entrance whose double doors had been replaced by draperies constructed from a pair of the king's voluminous silk trousers.

This apartment, Sing Tow's home, which he shared with his owners and a Vietnamese manservant, was always overflowing with interesting visitors. By day, they sat for hours in the formal dining room or on chairs and love seats in the drawing room. At night, the furniture was moved aside by the manservant. Cushions were placed on the floor and brightly colored but frayed silk kimono were brought out for an ever-changing cast of characters who spent hours, and occasionally even days, absorbed in intense conversation.

Most of the old people had spent months or years in internment camps in Europe or Asia. The conversation turned to the meaning of life and death, of war and peace, of the morality of almost any imaginable activity, including the eating of animals and, *in extremis,* people. Sing Tow surveyed this samsaric scene from a large silk pillow in front of one of the French doors, which gave onto a balcony overlooking the rue de Lille. He gravely accepted bits of fruit or petit pain that guests felt moved to share with him.

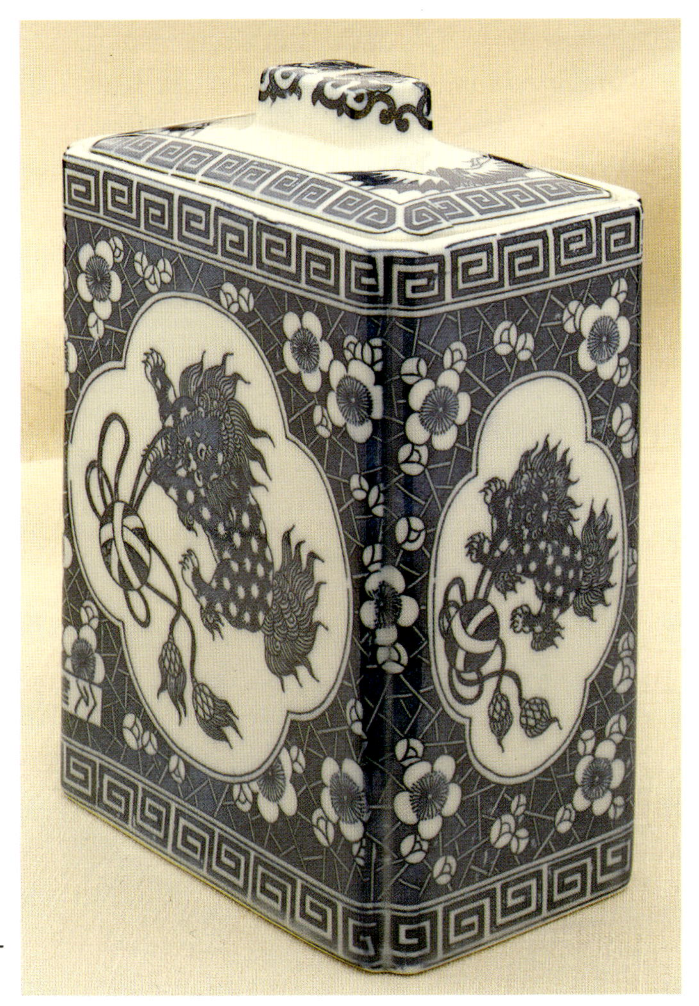

5. *A Chinese porcelain tea caddy deco-rated with Fo dogs.*

Sing Tow, his idiosyncratic master and mistress, and probably most of the other people we met in that apartment in Paris left this world a very few years after our visit. Nevertheless, absorbing memories of the interesting ménage in the rue de Lille, of the lengthy ruminations on Eastern, particularly Buddhist, philosophy, of the engaging Sing Tow, and of the exceptional collection of Asian carvings have remained with me these many years.

The great dog-lion, as well as his extension, the small lion-dog, is known as *shih tzu* (*shi zi*) in Chinese, shishi or kara-shishi in Japanese, *kang seng* in Tibetan, *su tu* in Vietnamese, and, as already observed, sing tow in Thai. In the first chapter, the history of the flesh-and-blood dog of Buddha will be examined. This faithful guardian of bed and hearth was married to the legendary dog-lion by Asian artists inspired by a Buddhist muse and a vision of the spiritual unity of opposites.

THE LION-DOG
OF BUDDHIST ASIA

FLESH-AND-FUR LION-DOGS

The Shih Tzu is one type of small, "short-headed" (that is, flat-faced), short-legged canine once known in China as an "under the table dog." A small Shih Tzu is sometimes mistaken for a Pekingese, although he can be as large as his Lhasa Apso cousins. His ideal weight is thought to be between nine and eighteen pounds. He should not be more than ten and a half inches high at the withers, and should have a broad round head and large round eyes.

The Shih Tzu is expected to have a long, dense coat. Like the Pekingese, sometimes he is golden and has what is referred to as a black mask. He may be all black, brindle, gray, or gold, or a combination of any of these colors. It is usual for him to have coarse outer hair and profuse soft wool next to the skin, possibly inherited from Himalayan ancestors. The Shih Tzu's Tibetan forebears were known as "sleeping dogs," since they made very cosy bed companions for a chilly night.

The characteristic which distinguishes the Shih Tzu from other flat-faced dogs is the "chrysanthemum" distribution of his facial hair. Like the Lhasa's, his hair grows profusely from his almost nonexistent nose and around his eyes. Unlike the Lhasa's, however, the Shih Tzu's hair is not usually allowed to fall naturally and to camouflage his face. On adult dogs, the uncut hair of head and forehead is caught up in a topknot. Adult dogs not destined for the show ring, as well as very young dogs and puppies, may have the hair on muzzle and forehead trimmed to give the appearance of the petals of the chrysanthemum flower. Some Shih Tzu with hair trimmed short on their faces clearly reveal their Pekingese antecedents.

An intimate relationship with humans is the most outstanding feature of the little lion-dog. He cherishes humans and craves their companionship. The Chinese thought of him as not wholly canine. The Japanese called their lion-dog the Chin, a creature part dog, part human, part spirit.

The earliest "under the table dog" was probably a short-

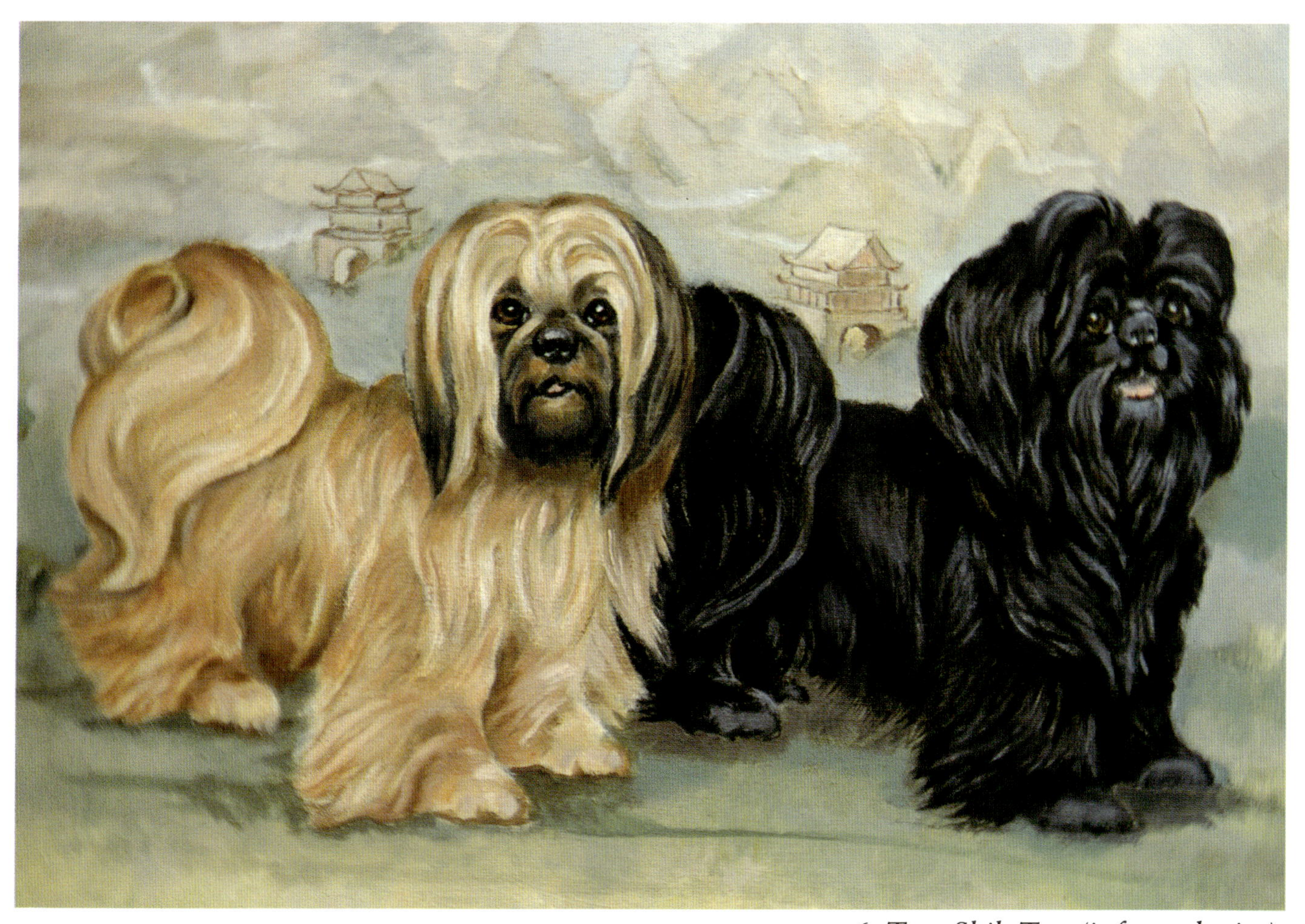

6. *Two Shih Tzu (informal trim).*

legged ancestor of the Chinese Pug, and may have existed as early as the Zhou dynasty (ca. 1123–256 B.C.). Between the eighth and mid-eleventh centuries A.D. he seems to have been in residence at the Chinese court. Around the middle of the eleventh century a Chinese official wrote: "In Ssechuan [Sichuan] there is a place named Lo-chiang [Luoqiang], famous for its dogs. Such as these are very quick of ear, and should be bred in the palace so as to give early warning of trouble outside."

During the Song dynasty (960–1279), around the year 990, the emperor Tai Zong was presented with a "Luoqiang dog," whom the emperor named Tao Hua, or Peach-flower. This dog was very intelligent and completely devoted to his imperial owner, from whom he was never separated. Peach-flower preceded the emperor to the audience chamber, announcing the imperial arrival with a bark. When, in the course of things, the emperor fell ill, Peach-flower would not eat. When the emperor died, Peach-flower cried inconsolably. The little dog could not be persuaded by the court eunuchs to serve the new emperor, Shen Zong. Finally the emperor had the grieving dog placed in a cage with white cushions, a sign of mourning, and carried in the imperial chair to his late master's tomb. There Peach-flower died, was wrapped in the cloth of an imperial umbrella, and was buried beside his master.

The short-headed "under the table dog" was not the only canine creature favored and cultivated in China. A hundred years
before the Christian era, a flourishing trade between Rome and
the Far East brought tiny Maltese dogs to Asia in exchange for
silks. A sixteenth-century writer described this breed as "dogges
curled and rough all over, which by reason of the length of their
haire makes show neither of face nor of body." About two hundred years later another writer maintained that the Maltese
might be short-haired, long-haired, or maned. The dogs of
Malta were prized in China both for their diminutive size and
for their intelligence. Almost certainly, they were frequently bred
to the flat-faced Chinese Pugs.

A pair of tiny Maltese dogs were sent from Constantinople
to the Chinese court during the Tang dynasty (618–907). The
dogs may have weighed under three pounds, and certainly
weighed no more than seven. These intrepid creatures were able
to lead horses by their reins. At night they carried flaming
torches in their mouths to light the imperial path.

The history of any breed of dog in the Far East is veiled in
the mists of time and change. At least one authority on canine
history maintains that all Chinese and Tibetan house dogs are
closely related, since they have common ancestors and frequently have been interbred. Breeding was not carried out in ac-

cordance with written standards, and many matches were made to increase or decrease size or to affect color and markings or length and density of coat—or simply to cater to imperial whim.

"Sleeve dogs," the most diminutive of the Pekingese type, were cultivated in China principally during the reign of Dao Guang, from 1821 to 1851. During that period the Manchu aristocracy in Beijing sent gifts to relatives in Manchuria, resulting in considerable prosperity in that region. One indication of this prosperity and of the prevalence of luxury was the proliferation of tiny pet dogs. The "sleeve dogs" were stunted specimens of many breeds, and the dwarf dogs remained popular in Manchuria even after they were no longer in favor at the Chinese court. As late as the early twentieth century, tiny dogs could be found in Heilongjiang, a province of northeastern China bordering Korea and the Soviet Union. They were called lion-dogs, and were taught to do all sorts of tricks for their owners' amusement. Since the Chinese were inclined to call many shaggy canines with broad faces lion-dogs, it cannot be surmised whether these dwarfs more closely resembled the present-day Japanese Chin or the Shih Tzu. In Beijing, miniature dogs have been rare since the mid-nineteenth century, because the Empress Dowager Ci Xi (r. 1861–1908) disapproved of the practice of dwarfing dogs.

At the opposite extreme of the size spectrum, in the 1940s

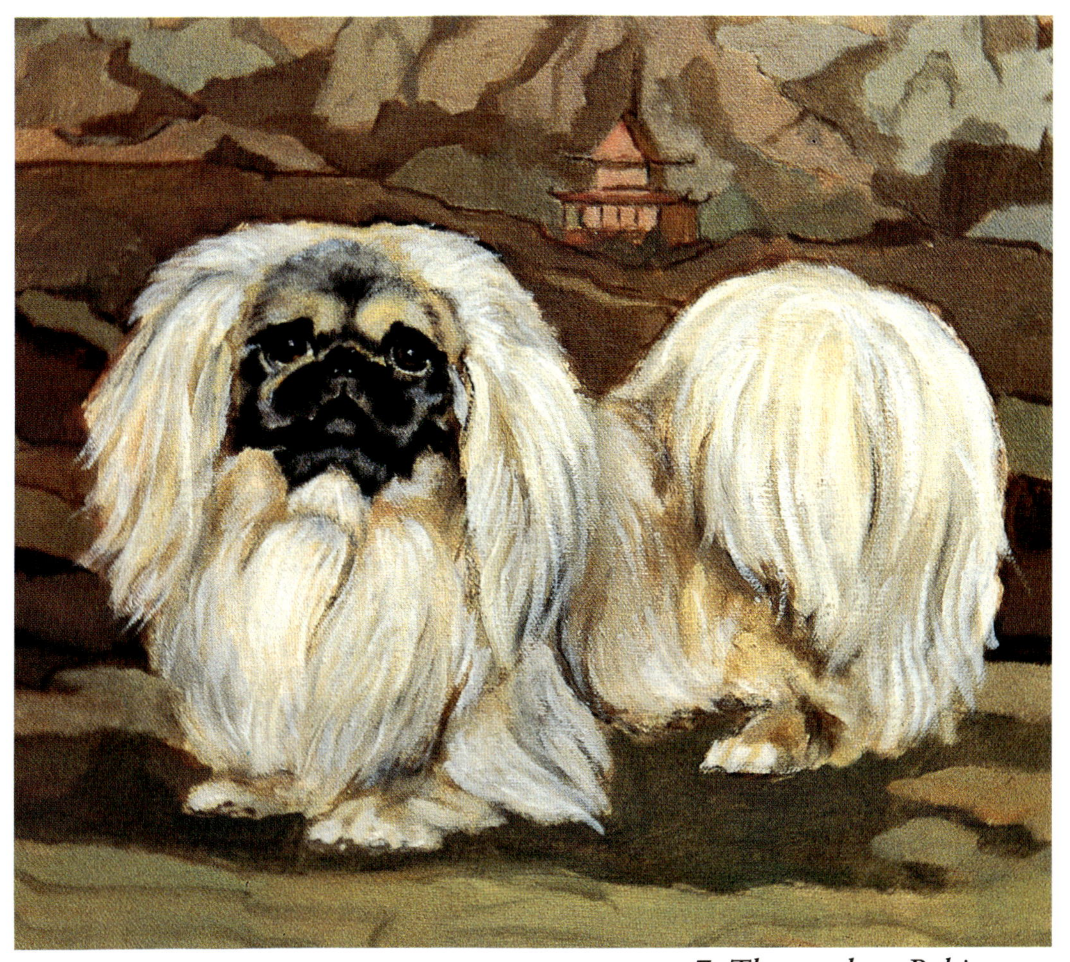

7. The modern Pekingese.

there appeared in a Massachusetts dog show an extraordinary giant fifty-pound Pekingese, a splendidly leonine creature who stood about twenty inches at the withers and was about three feet in length. A true Pekingese in every respect except size, this monster was said to be a guard dog, capable of apprehending intruders with his heavy lower jaw and well-developed fangs.

When Marco Polo was in China during the Yuan dynasty (1270–1368), he observed "lions" in the palace courtyards and noted: "These beasts were small and short of body, but they are astonishingly like the golden-coated nimble dogs which the people bred in their homes." One cannot help wondering if the creatures he saw might have been giant lion-dogs rather than actual lions.

The dog now known as the Pekingese became an established breed in England in 1895 with the creation of the Japanese and Pekingese Club. In 1904 the Pekingese and the Japanese Spaniel, now known in the United States as the Japanese Chin, were separated, and thereafter each evolved as a separate breed.

The Japanese Chin, first seen in Japan in the seventh century, has thin, silky hair and longer, straighter legs than the modern Pekingese. The Pekingese exhibited in present-day dog shows has very short, bowed legs and a dense undercoat. This is quite a different dog from the winner in English show rings during the

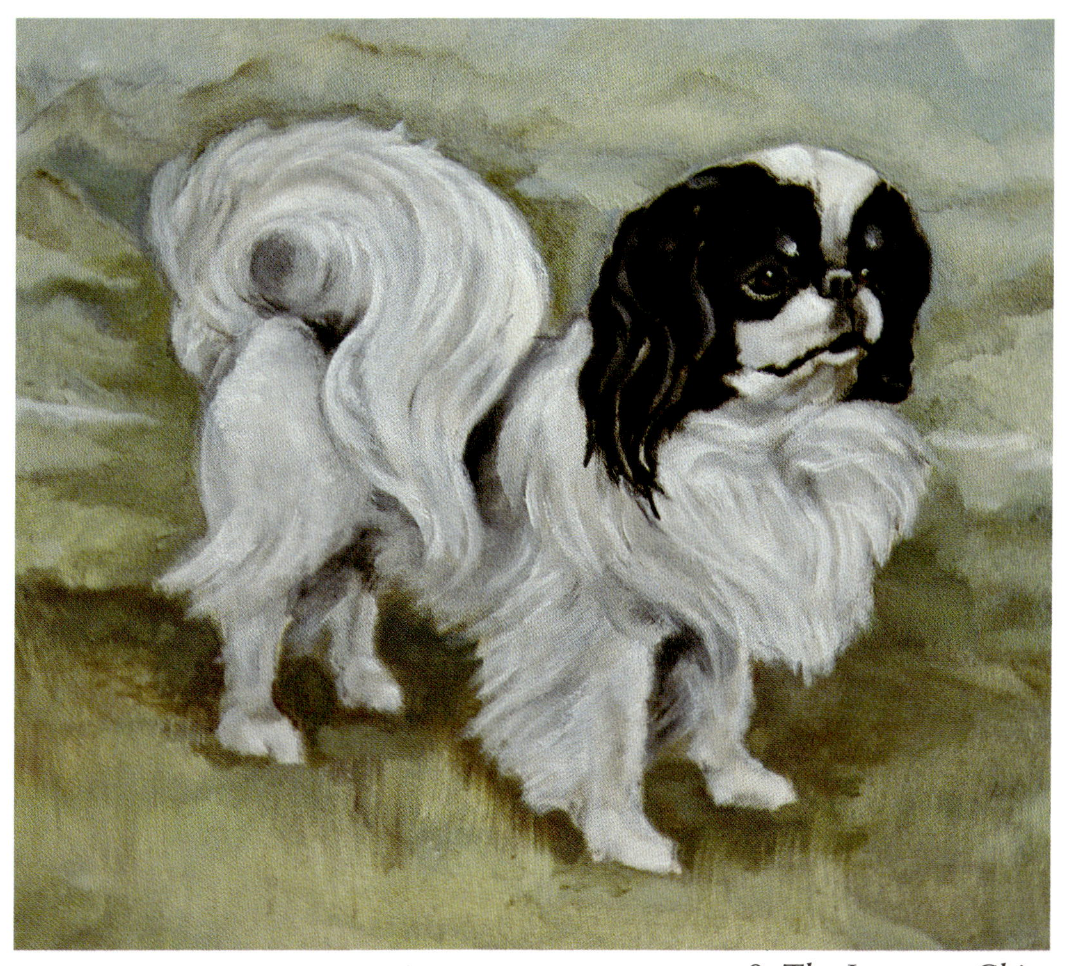

8. The Japanese Chin.

early part of this century. Examples of prize winners of that time may be seen at the Zoological Museum in Tring, Hertfordshire, England, now a branch of the British Museum (Natural History). Here former show winners and pets have been stuffed and mounted. These carefully preserved creatures include numerous small, flat-faced dogs. One Pekingese presented to the museum in 1923 bears a strong resemblance to small Shih Tzu seen in England a few years later.

Now let us return to the Tang dynasty, when there was considerable intercourse between China and Tibet. In the mid-seventh century a Chinese princess was sent as a bride to the Tibetan king, and it is possible that she was accompanied by several "under the table dogs." Perhaps because of the altitude, it was found wise to unite the Chinese lap dogs with smaller specimens of the heavy-coated, longer-nosed Tibetan dogs, traditionally cherished in the homes, palaces, and monasteries of the Himalayas. These canine companions of the mountain people of Tibet were cheerful, loving, and sturdy. Alliances between the happy-go-lucky dogs of Lhasa (Lhasa Apsos) and the ornamental silken Chinese aristocrats with their flower-shaped faces probably took place first in Tibet, then in China. The second generation of "under the table dogs" in Tibet may not have been very different from the Lhasa Apso. In China the second or third

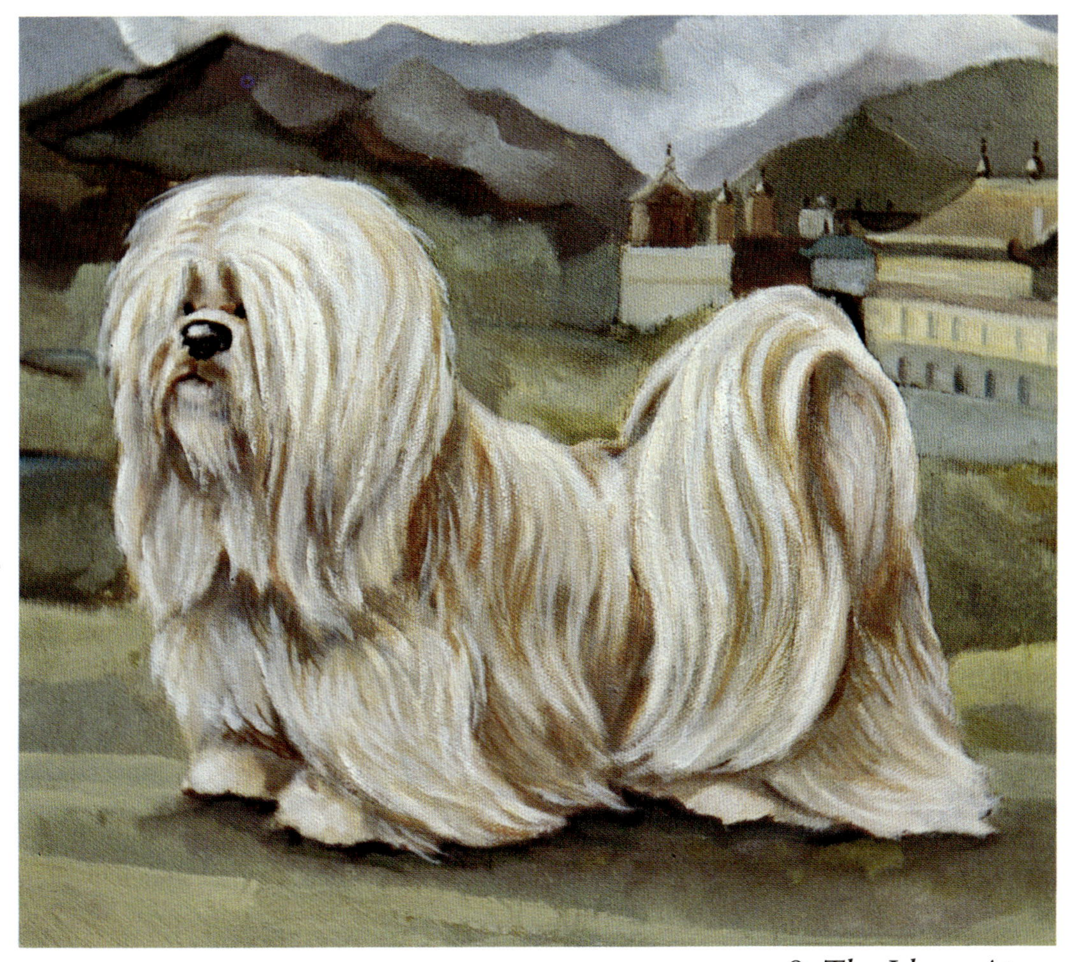

9. The Lhasa Apso.

generation of "little lions" chosen to propagate their kind were probably hardly distinguishable from other flat-faced dogs with prominent eyes except for their remarkably heavy coats and the chrysanthemum distribution of hair on their faces.

The Chinese believed that the Shih Tzu's origins were in Tibet. However, the flat faces and short noses of the Shih Tzu were not characteristic of the native dogs, whose respiratory apparatus was more appropriate to the Tibetan altitudes. The Chinese imperial court received lion-dogs from the Dalai Lama in 1645, and then again in 1653, when the Dalai Lama visited the emperor in Beijing. These gifts were probably small Lhasa Apsos. More than two hundred years later, in 1908, the Empress Dowager received a small Lhasa Apso closely resembling a Shih Tzu when another Dalai Lama visited the Chinese court.

The Lhasa Apso, about whom more will be said in chapter five, was not only a "sleeping dog," that is, a bed companion, in his native land. He was also a frequent companion of lamas, the revered religious teachers of Tibetan Buddhism. He was bred in monasteries and sold to nomads as a mascot. He also made himself useful in temple life by learning to turn the ubiquitous prayer wheels. The wheels were actually cylindrical drums containing Buddhist sutras, or scriptures. Each revolution of the container was believed to add to the store of good karma in the world. The wheels were beacons of hope for believers in the Buddha's teaching, and perhaps they also brought good karma to the Shih Tzu's ancestors who diligently kept the religious engines in motion.

Possibly the reader has become confused by the tangled skein of ancestors and antecedents. It is not easy to reconstruct a history based on pictures in imperial record books, a tradition of legends and anecdotes taken from ancient texts, and the evidence of paintings and sculptures executed over a period of nearly two thousand years. The would-be historian or genealogist is left with questions and puzzles that cannot be answered or resolved. However, it is definitely known that from the earliest times, and in every Asian country where there were some means and leisure, small lion-dogs of various kinds whose only function was companionship were cultivated and prized.

The lion-dog's ancestors endured long and dangerous voyages by land and by sea, savage massacres, famines, and devastating plagues. Throughout the ages, their human admirers have found it worthwhile to ensure their survival. However, in the East as in the West, the canine species has not always been dealt with in a way on which the human race can congratulate itself. Humanity has not proved its oft-vaunted superiority by compassion or even reason. Dogs have been stimulated and goaded to fight each other and to hunt down other animals. Some humans maintain that if a creature is "only an animal" its sensibilities are of no consequence, or are even nonexistent.

It is the way of the world and of what Buddhists call Samsara, the realm of birth, death, and rebirth, that both man and dog are prone to eating other animals, occasionally including each other. Actually, except in times of famine, there is more often a man-eat-dog situation than the reverse. At various times and places men have fancied and continue to fancy not only cattle and pigs but also creatures as varied as caterpillars, snakes, mice, rats, and cats, as well as canines. Even in North America, dog meat was found in public markets into the early nineteenth century. The Chinese and Koreans have always preyed and fed on the canine species. A nineteenth-century Western traveler remarked on placards posted on many Chinese Buddhist temples asking people to please refrain from eating the flesh of animals, particularly the dog, who is the faithful guardian of his master's home.

The Japanese, especially the common people, have not always been known for their benevolence to dogs. However, within historical times they have never put dogs on the menu. Some have questioned the ability of religion to sway the behavior of adherents. Probably the dog's lot has been made easier by teachings of compassion, though the wish to avoid punishment

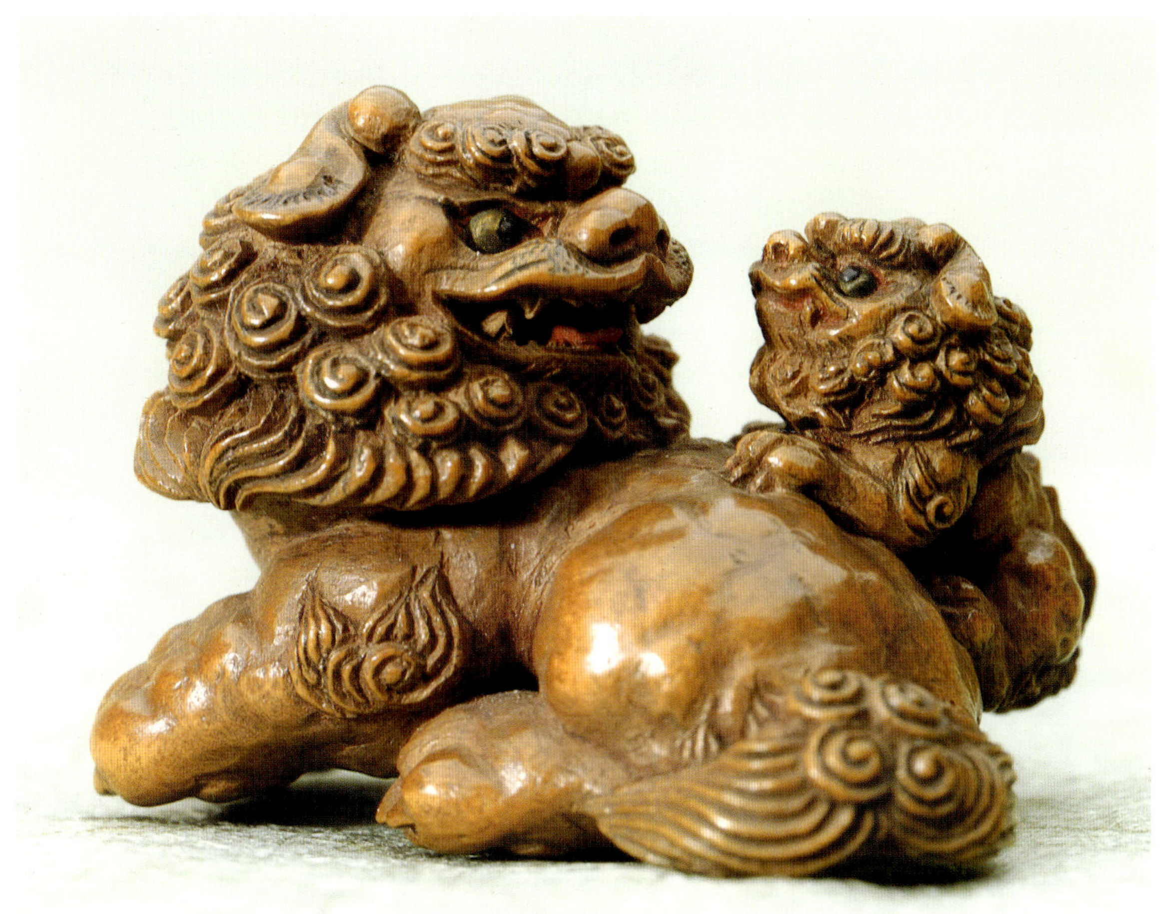

10. A wood netsuke mother shishi and offspring.

in an afterlife may have done more to smooth his path through human history. This question of the relationship of the two-legged and the four-legged will be dealt with in more detail in chapter six.

Generally, the lion-dogs have been more fortunate than many larger Asian canines. In Asia their human protectors treasured them and cared for them well. Before the communist era, the Chinese utilized different kinds of dogs for different functions. There were fighting dogs, guard dogs, small companion dogs, and the terribly unfortunate edible dogs. Since the advent of communism, there are probably few small companion dogs left on mainland China. Large guard dogs may be valued members of the family in some parts of the countryside, where they share family meals. However, dogs are not supposed to be kept in the cities, and smaller dogs are always in danger of ending their lives as a human's dinner.

The Shih Tzu arrived in the West—in Scandinavia, England, and Ireland—in the late 1920s and early 1930s. In 1938 the first Shih Tzu were exported from England to the United States, where they were registered as Lhasa Apsos. The American Kennel Club did not recognize the Shih Tzu as a separate breed until the early 1950s. In 1969 they were finally permitted registration in the AKC stud book.

The first arrivals in the United States were blessed with appreciative humans who went to considerable pains to see to their well-being. Recently, as their popularity has grown, their numbers have greatly increased. A population explosion has been created by irresponsible breeders and puppy mills. They flood pet shops with sickly, neurotic puppies and are responsible for many having their short lives ended in city pounds or in the homes of people too insensitive and self-absorbed to care for them properly. Sometimes they are presented to the human young as an animated toy, but this is rarely a successful enterprise. Usually children must be taught gentleness and respect. They are often too rough and thoughtless to care for small dogs.

Why have the Shih Tzu and other small dogs of East Asia survived these many centuries in a world where utility to humans would seem to have been an essential ingredient of their survival? Fortunately, men's psyches seem to have a special compartment from which emanates a love for such unlikely phenomena as violets, ladybugs, hummingbirds, and small, dependent four-legged beings. Even those humans who do not need lion-dogs to carry lighted torches to illuminate dark paths, to turn prayer wheels, to amuse their children, or to announce visitors may become beguiled and love them with the same love they bestow upon their human friends.

CHAPTER TWO

LIONS AND DOG-LIONS

Why do lions guard the banks in Hong Kong? Evil spirits dare not pass these stern stone guardians which protect banks, businesses and private houses." So runs an advertisement by the Hong Kong Tourist Association in the *New Yorker* magazine. Above the advertisement is a sketch of a benevolent, smiling temple lion. His eyebrows in the form of stylized Chinese clouds, a red ribbon with a rosette around his neck, and a ball under his paw, he smiles mischievously out at the reader. Many admirers of the Shih Tzu will realize that this cheery fellow is as much dog as lion. In fact it is only the dog-lion who smiles. True lions are solemn, imposing creatures, without any inclination to levity.

There was a time when Chinese dog-lion images flanking doorways were permitted by law only in front of temples and official buildings. The size of the guardian creatures indicated the importance of the building and of its function. In China the earliest example of doorway guardians seems to have been the palace of a man who died in 117 B.C. The custom was well established by the Tang dynasty.

Today, dog-lions in front of Buddhist temples and other buildings are usually arranged so that the male, recognizable by the ball under his front paw, is situated in the east, while his mate, a baby under her paw, is in the west. The east is relegated to the influence of the male, or *yang,* and the west to that of the female, or *yin.*

Occasionally, a dog-lion pair is distinguished by an added feature. The male is open-mouthed, while his mate's mouth is tightly closed. Since they are Buddhist beings, together they silently but plainly emit the sacred mantric syllable *aum.* The male commences with *au,* and the female completes the mantra with her mouth closed: *mmm.*

Traditionally, the king of the beasts inspired both Buddhists and Christians to think of the founders of their respective religions as lions. Sometimes the lion represented Christ himself to early medieval Christians. Buddhists attributed certain leonine

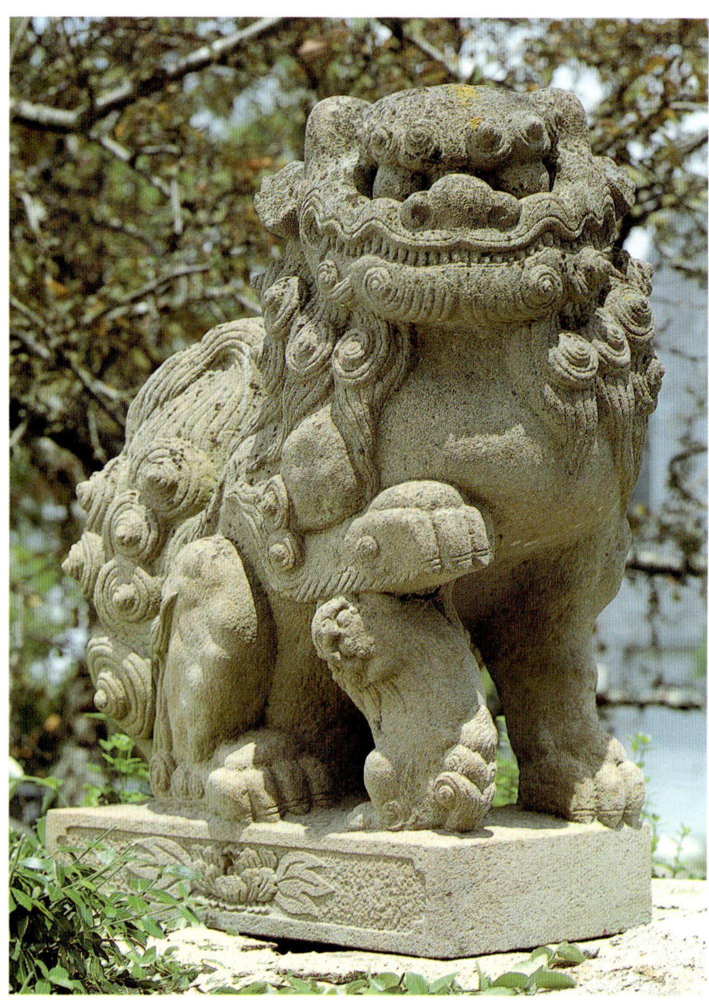

11. *The female partner of a pair of stone dog-lions from China.*

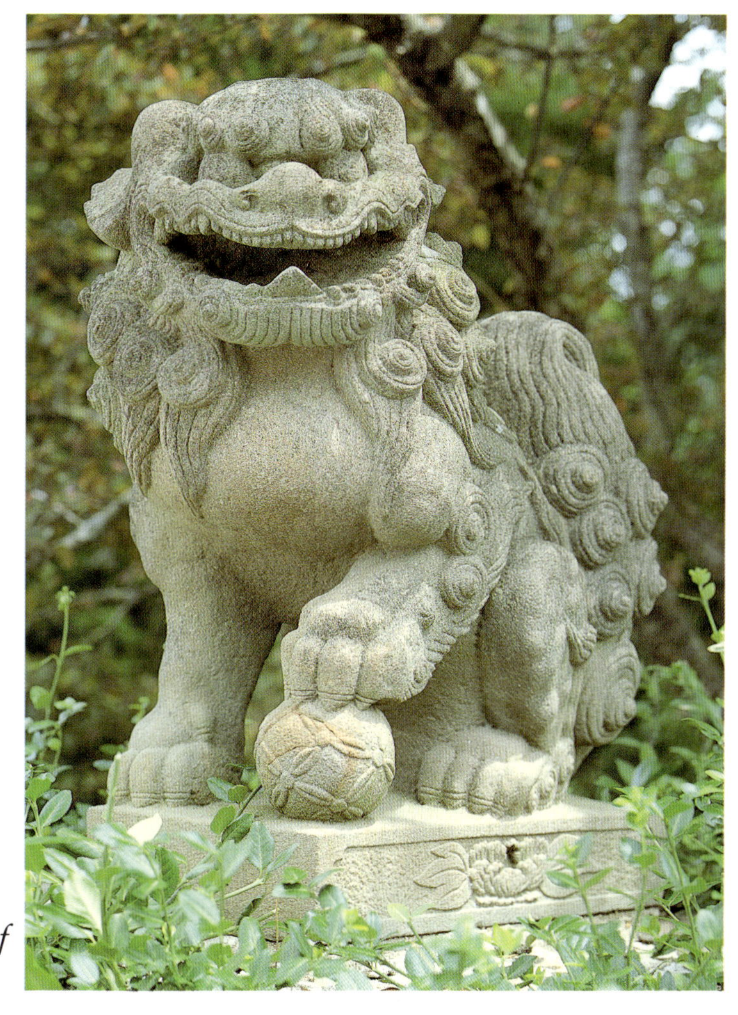

12. *The male partner of a pair of stone dog-lions from China.*

characteristics to the Buddha's appearance. Their spirit-lions, in turn, borrowed some physical attributes, including periwinkle curls, from images of the Enlightened One. According to legend, the Buddha sat so long and so still in meditation that snails took up residence on his head, thereby inspiring generations of artists to adorn both Buddha and dog-lion images with the same snail-like curls.

There are two types of Chinese Buddhist lions. Both greatly resemble what most Westerners think of as the Pekingese; they have prominent eyes, short noses, and wispy, cloudlike strands of hair floating from their chins, the backs of their forelegs, and their heels. The first sort of lion is a single figure with no orna-mentation or only a simple collar and bell. On the other hand, lion pairs with offspring are usually embellished with ornate openwork or flower-trimmed harnesses draped loosely around their necks. From under their profuse manes emerge flat cords trimmed with loops or bows that fall down the middle of the back, terminating at the tail. Tassels and bells dangle from the harness. Sometimes decorative lion heads are affixed to the crea-tures' chests, and large tassels hang from the mouths of these or-naments.

These elaborate decorations were the imaginative creations of Tibetan lamas in China, for whom the lion was the most im-

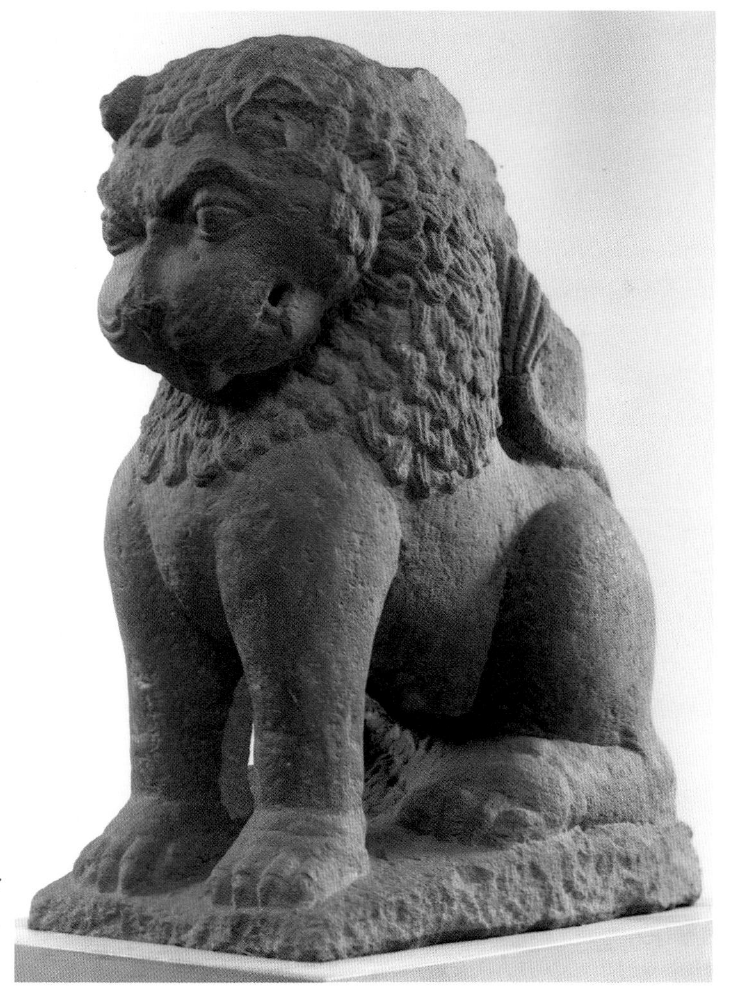

13. *An Indian stone lion; fifth or sixth century* A.D. *Courtesy, Museum of Fine Arts, Boston; bequest of Charles Ames Cummings.*

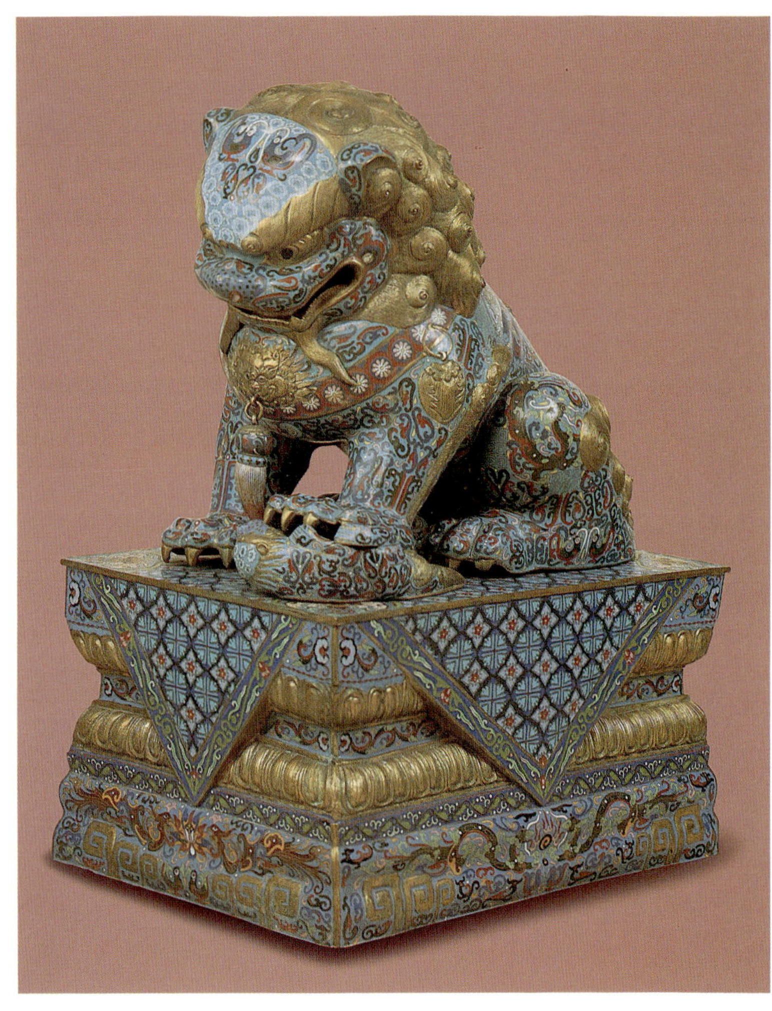

14. *The female partner of a pair of cloisonné Fo lions from China.*

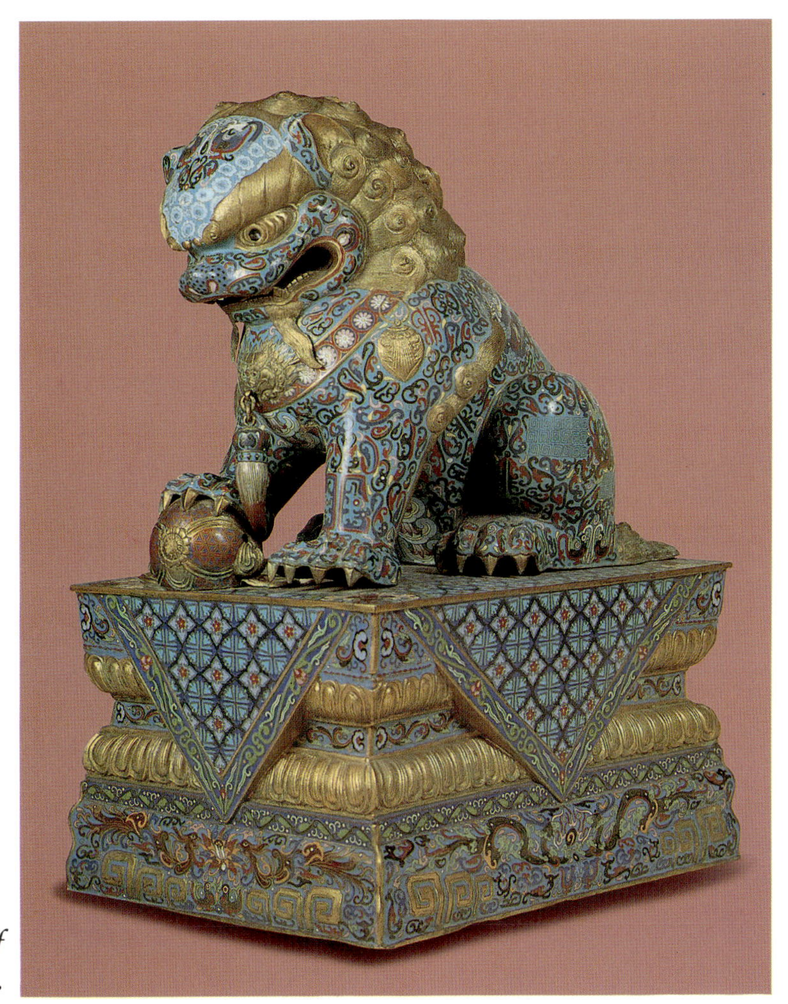

15. *The male partner of a pair of cloisonné Fo lions from China.*

portant symbol, and companion, of the Lord Buddha. The harness symbolizes the subjection of strength and courage to the service of the Enlightened One, and to what Buddhists call the buddha-nature.

A variation of the guardian dog-lion is found in Japan inside Buddhist temples and before Shinto shrines. In Nikko the tomb of Tokugawa Ieyasu, the first shogun of the Edo period (1603–1868), is protected by pairs of *koma-inu,* or "Korean dogs," as the Japanese call this creature. Buddhism reached Japan by way of Korea, and possibly this is the origin of the appellation. On the other hand, the Japanese refer to the Chinese form of the dog-lion as the *kara-shishi,* or "Chinese dog-lion." The Korean dogs have no babies or decorative balls, and no elaborate trappings of harness, bells, or tassels, such as are found on the guardian Fo dogs of China. The bodies of the Korean dogs are not as massively compact as those of their Chinese counterparts. Their rather long forelegs are stretched out firmly and straight in front of them.

At the thirteenth-century Japanese temple Eihei-ji, in Fukui Prefecture, the Hatto, or teaching hall, contains four Korean dogs which are probably of quite recent manufacture. Also known as *ama-inu,* "dogs of heaven," they are situated cater-corner on either side of the foot of the altar. They are brightly painted and wear broad smiles. They add a whimsical touch to an elaborate and formal religious setting, even as stone gargoyles provide fanciful ornamentation to the cathedral of Notre Dame, in Paris. Ancient spiritual traditions have a mature and sophisticated wisdom which inspires cultural expressions of wit and fancy. The Shih Tzu may be said to be a living expression of that Buddhist whimsy.

Some Indian Buddhist lions resemble the living creature, but others are rather peculiar from a strictly zoological point of view. Thus at Sarnath, where the Buddha preached his first sermon, a lion pillar is topped by four quite lifelike lions. However, their manes have stylized short waves, and viewed head-on, their faces are all smiling benevolence. Erected about 250 B.C., this early work of Buddhist art is the emblem of the present-day Republic of India.

A lion, more or less stylized, ornaments the national flag of Sri Lanka. In Burma, the great temple guardians resemble stylized panthers, and the Vietnamese Buddhist lion, or *su tu*, as he is called there, bears a resemblance to the koma-inu. One bronze temple lion (*sing tow*) from Thailand, photographed for a decorators' magazine, has a square jaw and large, round eyes of pink quartz. With his long, straight forelegs, he too resembles the koma-inu. He and the little ball which he holds under one paw

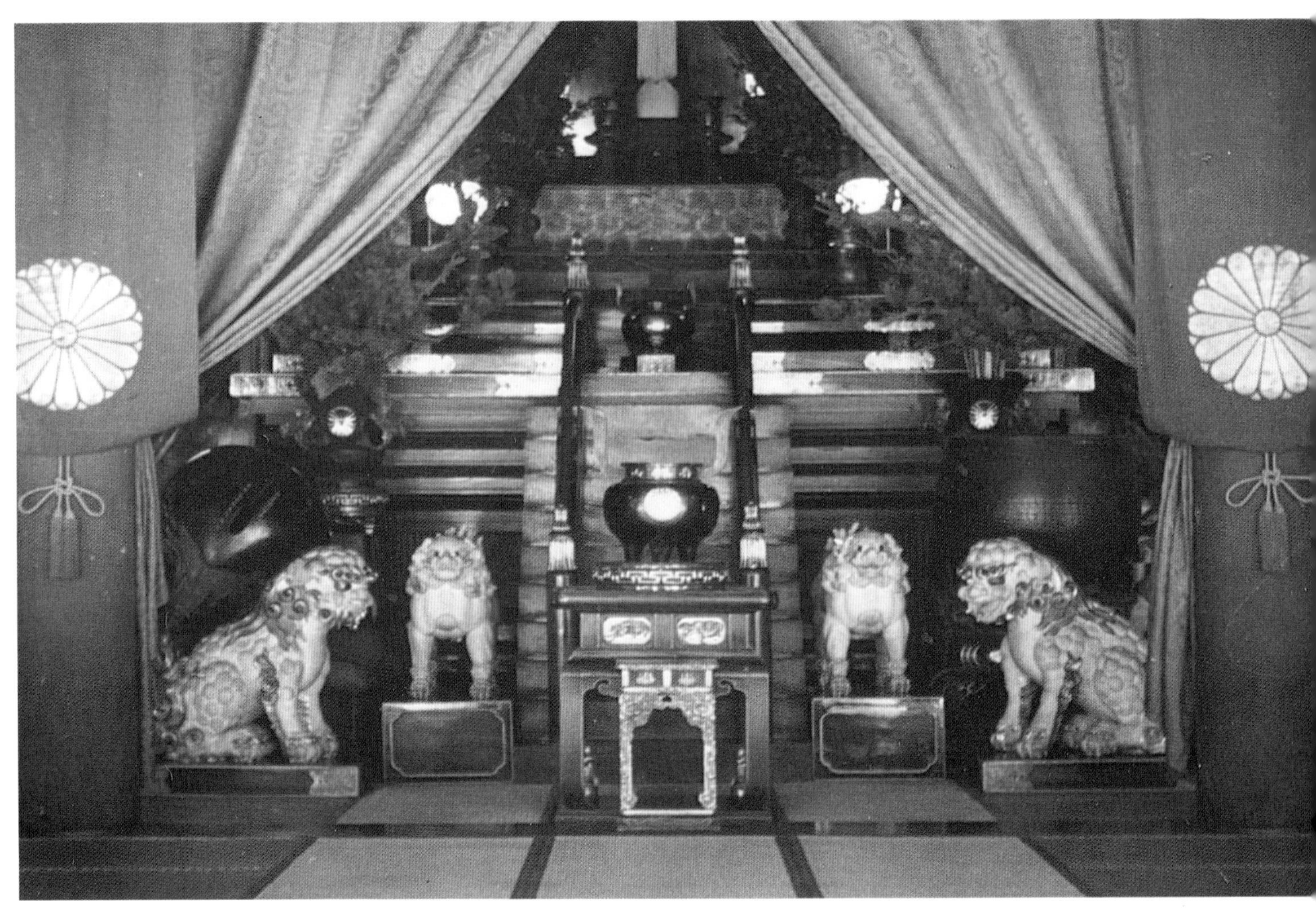

54 THE LION-DOG OF BUDDHIST ASIA

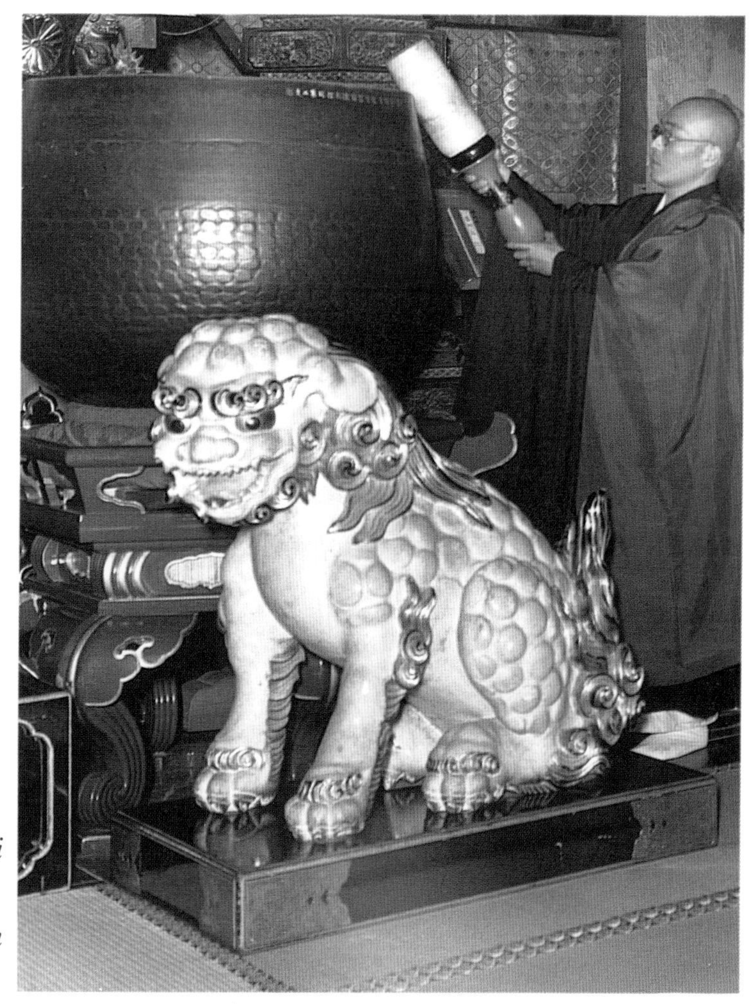

16 (opposite). *Koma-inu at Eihei-ji temple, Japan.*

17. *One of the koma-inu seen in plate 16.*

are decorated with primitive colored glass insets forming stylized flower and cloud designs.

The following Chinese lamaist legend recounted by the scholar V. W. F. Collier is one Buddhist explanation for the stationing of guardian beings at the entrances of temples. According to this legend, one day the Buddha arrived before his temple, paused before entering, and commanded his great dog-lion companions to remain at the entrance until his return. Tables covered with altar cloths were brought. Such altar tables were often used as seats by Tibetan religious teachers when they preached. Each guardian creature climbed aboard a table, there to wait in motionless obedience to the Buddha's word. They still await their master, silently conveying their own teaching of patience and of the subjection of their egos and passions to the Buddhist Dharma.

Another anecdote related by Collier indicates the steadfastness expected by Chinese lamaists of the guardian dog-lions of Fo. In the spring of 1916 a pair of stone lions was to be moved from a palace in the eastern end of Beijing to a different location in another part of the imperial city. One of the creatures could not be removed from his seat despite considerable effort. Finally a Buddhist priest was fetched. The priest made an offering of wine, placed a yellow paper with mantric characters on the lion's breast, and bound his eyes with a red cloth. As a result of these ministrations, the lion was persuaded to descend from his pedestal and allowed himself to be transported and installed in the new location.

Steadfastness and subjection of ego were not the only qualities expected of the Buddha's dog-lions. Dog-lion babies were put through a rigorous endurance test by their mother. Like Japanese mountain ascetics, her offspring were required to prove their strength and determination, their worthiness to become dogs of Buddha. The mother dog-lion carried her children to the top of a steep precipice, and there she duly pushed them, one by one, over the edge. The little creatures were expected to clamber back up the difficult slope to rejoin their parent, thereby giving proof of their capacity to function as dog-lions of Fo.

As already pointed out, in China dog-lion guardians were placed before entrances and temple altars. They also resided on altars erected in peoples' homes, and smaller versions were stationed on the roof corners of temples. The last custom seems to have originated in the Tang dynasty, and was thought to protect the temple from fire.

Centuries before the writing of characters appeared in China, the lion was a hieroglyphic in Egypt. The Egyptians are believed to have worshiped the lion. Sacred lions, usually associated with the sun god, were kept in many parts of the country. The Egyptians believed that the sun god passed through the gates of dawn and evening each day. These gates were protected by lion gods.

The lion gods of Egypt were believed never to close their eyes when sleeping, and the Egyptians were persuaded that the king of the beasts, with his ever-open eyes, was the ultimate in creaturely protection. The Egyptians erected lion statues before palaces and tombs to ensure the safety of both the living and the dead.

The Egyptian sun deities Shu and his sister, Tefnut, were servants of the sun god. One was responsible for pushing the sun forward in order to make it rise, while the other supported the sun as it sank below the horizon. The equinoxes were orchestrated by the two lion gods, who pulled at ropes to maintain control. Chinese dog-lions are frequently represented as holding ropes or ribbons in their mouths. The ribbon usually emanates from a ball being guarded or played with by the dog-lions. Plates 22 and 23 show a good example of a family of dog-lions: a green jade mother and her two cubs playing with a broad ribbon. The ribbon is attached to a ball at one end and terminates in a large bow carved on the bottom of the statue.

Scholars can only speculate on the possibility of Egyptian

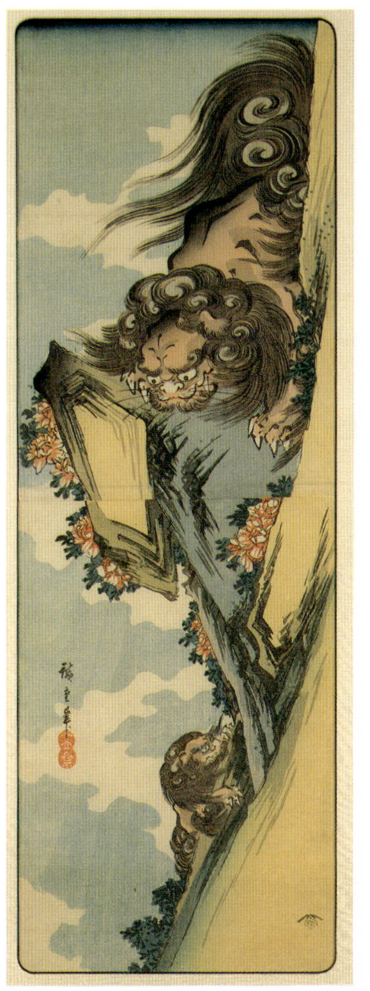

18. *A woodblock print of a mother shishi watch-ing her offspring scramble up a cliff.*

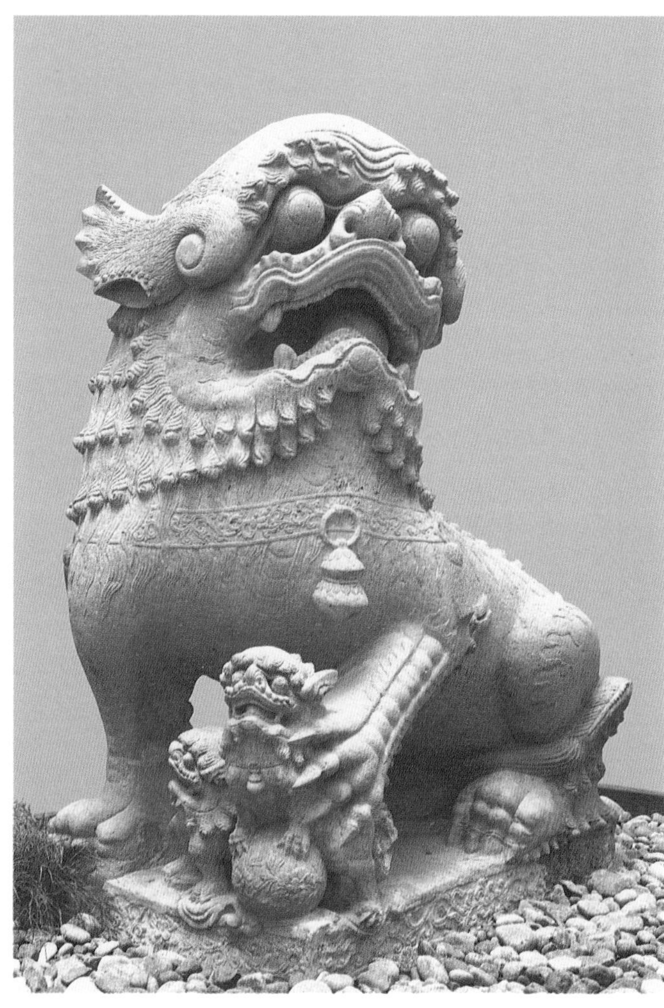

19. *The female partner of a pair of Chinese stone dog-lions with two offspring. Courtesy of the Peabody Museum of Salem.*

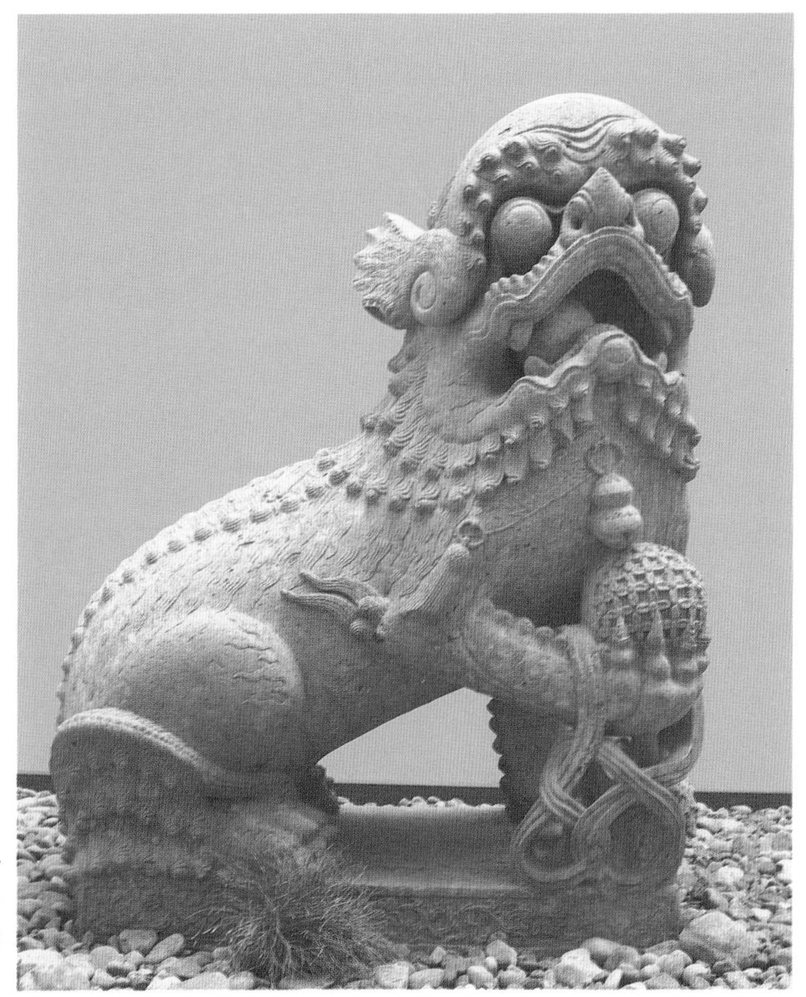

20. *The male partner of a pair of Chinese stone dog-lions with two offspring. Courtesy of the Peabody Museum of Salem.*

influence on the art and religious symbolism of East Asia. There are many interesting parallels, including the sun both as symbol and as deity. The Indo-Persians, early Buddhists, were also sun worshipers. The ball under the paw of the male dog-lion is thought to be a sun symbol as well as the symbol of the jewel of the Buddhist Dharma. The ball, according to legend, is hollow and symbolizes the "emptiness" of mind in Buddhist spirituality.

Heraldry in Europe goes back to the time of the Crusades. The lion, as symbol of strength and sometimes of Christ, was frequently incorporated into official and princely coats of arms in all European countries. Lions, usually realistically represented in stone or bronze, guard important buildings in European cities. However, early depictions and representations of lions occasionally were as fanciful as those of the dog-lions of Buddha. A twelfth-century Spanish lion fresco from the province of Burgos portrays a creature with a round, owllike face and with stylized curls on his head and neck. A small bronze German lion of only slightly later vintage (1200) is quite canine in appearance. His long thin legs are leonine, but his amiable doglike face and the curls of his mane and head do not suggest the real king of the beasts.

Medieval European authors of bestiaries attributed quite remarkable powers to the male lion. His progeny, born dead, remained without life for three days. On the third day their father "breathes in their faces and inspirits them." Lions stationed before church doors in Europe symbolized the Deity's watchfulness over his followers, and were the protectors of the sanctuary.

Christ and the founder of Buddhism were not the only spiritual entities to be identified with the lion. Saint Thomas the Apostle was traditionally associated with the royal creature. Saint Thomas, on a missionary venture in India, is said to have appeared astride a lion, accompanied by two dogs.

In Mahayana (Great Vehicle), or Northern, Buddhism there are numerous cosmic buddhas and bodhisattvas. A bodhisattva is a being who has put off the advent of his own enlightenment until everyone and everything in the universe, down to the last blade of grass, has become enlightened. One of these bodhisattvas is Manjusri. Manjusri is known as the guardian of spiritual wisdom. He is equipped with a sword with which he is prepared to slice through all illusions that cloud the minds of Buddhists and prevent them from realizing "the unborn, the unbecome, the unmade."

From this bodhisattva the Manchu dynasty of China (also known as the Qing dynasty; 1644–1911) took its name. Followers of lamaist Buddhism, the Manchus were Mongols, and their association with the bodhisattva Manjusri originated with the

Tibetan lamas. It has been suggested by a Chinese scholar that the gifts of small lion-dogs to the Manchu emperors by Tibetans symbolized a tribute of lions to Manjusri.

According to Chinese tradition, Manjusri was always accompanied by a small pet dog as he traveled about the countryside in the guise of a simple mendicant priest. One day while he was on his peregrinations a Daoist approached him. The Daoist, who did not recognize this meeting as an encounter with a bodhisattva, begged the mendicant to arrange an audience with Manjusri Bodhisattva for him. Manjusri took the Daoist to his dwelling and there presented him with tea and rice, after which the Daoist again begged for a vision of Manjusri. The Daoist was told he must rigorously observe the Buddhist precepts and that if he did so a vision of the bodhisattva would be forthcoming. At this, the Daoist protested vehemently that he always kept the religious precepts strictly. "If that is the case," replied Manjusri, "then look up into the sky." When the Daoist did as he was bidden, he perceived the pet dog transformed into an enormous lion, surrounded by colored lights and clouds aglow with five colors. On the back of the lion was the priest, now recognizable as Manjusri Bodhisattva. The fortunate Daoist had had an affinity with the bodhisattva from an earlier incarnation and was therefore enabled to perceive the celestial being.

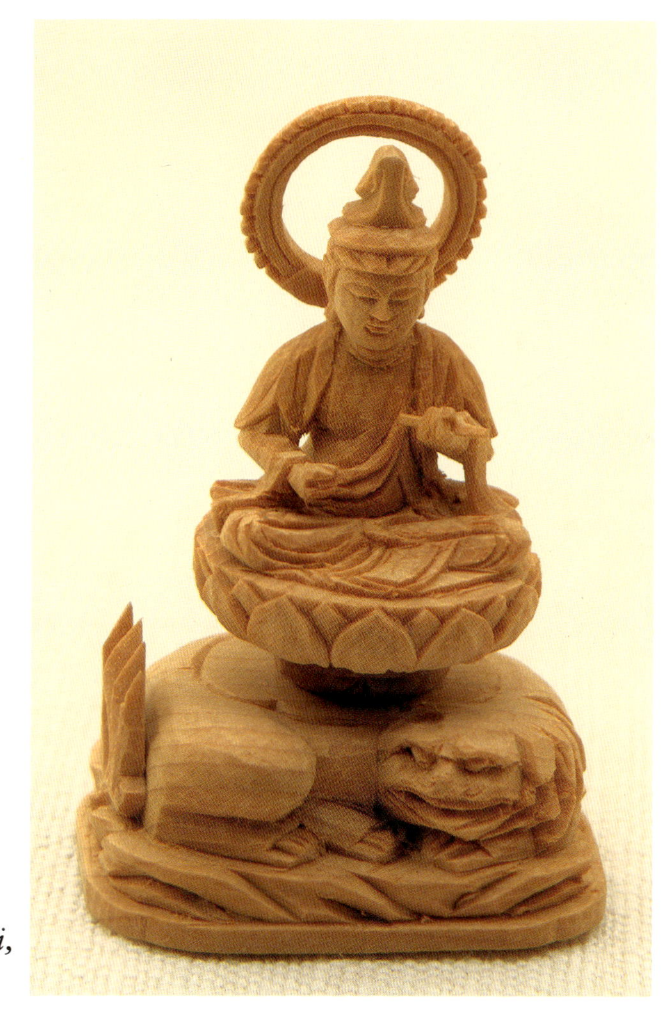

21. *A Japanese wood carving of Manjusri,
bodhisattva of wisdom, and his shishi.*

The reader may still have questions about the curious blending of the identities of dog and lion. Whence arose the desire to tame the king of the beasts, the symbol of courage, power, and authority, by infusion of a cosy canine symbol of companionship and loyalty? The question seems to contain its own answer. In ancient times, people could not find a way to exert power over a live lion, and power over a dead one could not have given any extended satisfaction. However, an infusion of canine camaraderie into feral ferocity produced a quite satisfying combination. The Chinese emperors discovered the pleasures both of taming the imperial symbol and of finding a loyal, affectionate friend.

Humans and dogs are animals with a tendency to gravitate toward a pack. However, even the most pack-dependent creature, two-legged or four-legged, knows, at least subconsciously, that the pack is capricious. An individual showing signs of weakness or idiosyncrasy may find the warmth and energies of the pack turned against him. Two-legged creatures then turn to their gods and bodhisattvas. A four-legged creature may turn to a two-legged being. The two-legged being who responds with an open heart discovers to his or her surprise that here is a small conduit to the eternal spirit which sustains all creatures, in good fortune and in adversity.

CHAPTER THREE

THE DOG OF FO AND THE JADE MYSTIQUE OF CHINA

It may interest students of Chinese art history that in China, with the exception of the dragon, no animal has been the subject of so many legends, and the object of so much symbolism, as the lion and the dog-lion. Originally, winged lions appeared as giant stone tomb guardians and as small stone artifacts for burial sites. Bronze lions were also common in early China. Most prized of all, from about the tenth century B.C. onward, were figures made of jade, a stone both precious and mystical to the Chinese since the dawn of their history. According to one early legend, axes made from this treasured mineral were forged

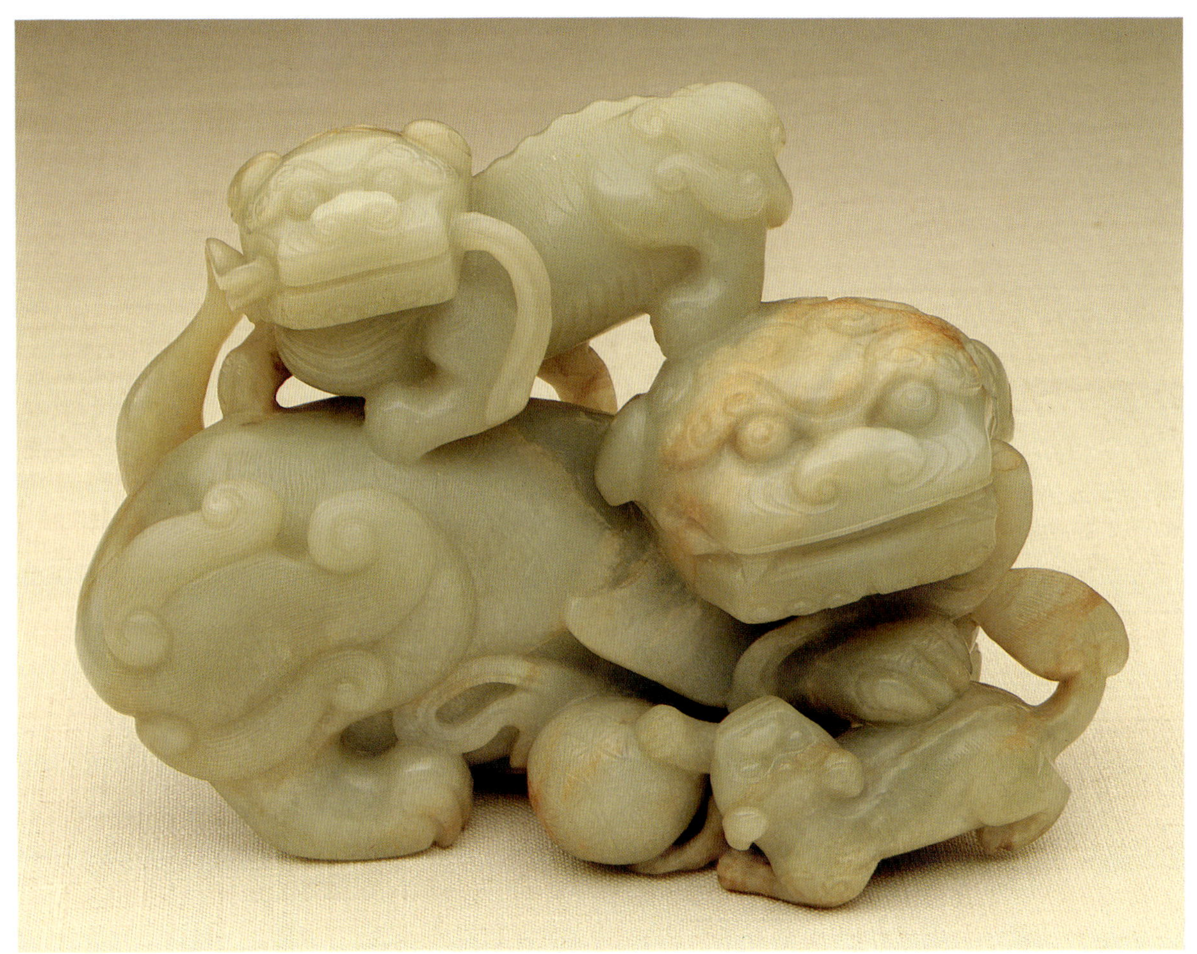

22. *A nephrite mother Fu dog and offspring.*

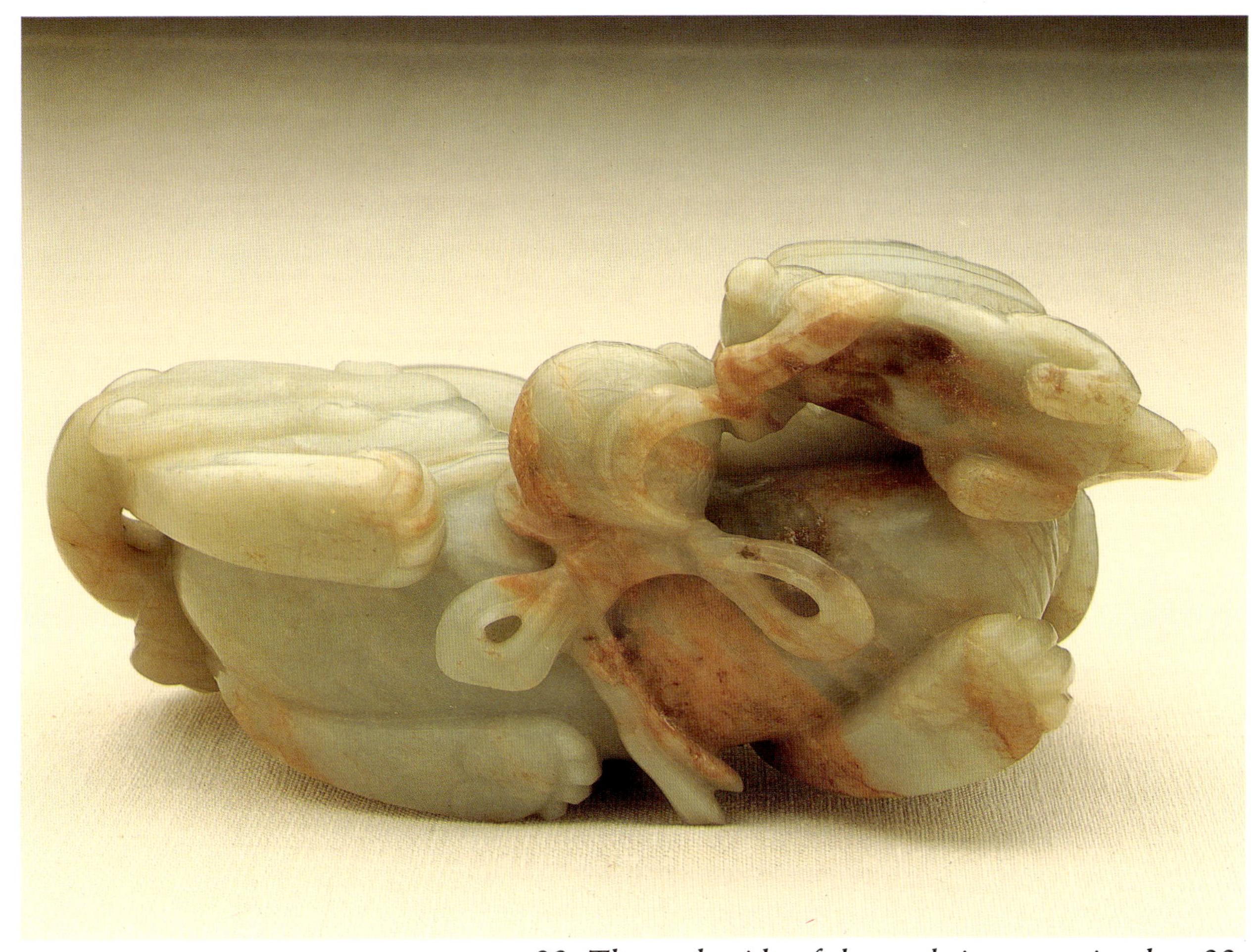

23. The underside of the nephrite group in plate 22.

from a rainbow by the storm god, then thrown to earth for man's use.

The stone casually referred to as jade is actually two different substances from separate sources. The first, jadeite, "is formed twenty to thirty miles below the surface of the earth," according to Richard Gump. "Nephrite," he continues "is formed closer to the earth's surface." It is nephrite that the Chinese have known and treasured throughout their history. From nephrite were made ritual ornaments, as well as the simple, elegant carvings of figures, animals, birds, and flowers of ancient China. Usually the jade artist is referred to as a carver, though actually jade is not carved but ground with the use of various abrasives. Among the jade creations were several different forms of dog-lions. The first dog-lions were squat, primitive figures, barely distinguishable from other mythical animals described later in this chapter.

Jadeite was introduced into China from Burma late in the seventeenth century and was never used for the ceremonial purposes of the Chinese court. Though jadeite is both heavier and harder than nephrite, the latter, according to Gump, is the world's toughest stone. Nephrite has a fibrous texture which requires great skill to work. Jadeite is granulated and therefore more inclined to fracture. It is crystalline, thus more brilliant and able to take a higher polish than nephrite, which is distinguished by a softer appearance. "Smash two diamonds together," writes Gump, "and one will break. Bring two pieces of nephrite together with all the force you can muster and the result will be only a loud sound; the stones will remain intact."

This "most completely Chinese of all materials" has been found outside the provinces of old Cathay since the beginning of Chinese recorded history. Historically, the source of nephrite was the riverbeds of Khotan-Yarkand. The first references to Khotan as the source of jade date back to the second century B.C. Khotan, located at an oasis in the Taklamakan desert, lies at the foot of the Kunlun mountains. From this range flow the Black Jade River and the River of White Jade, which carry nephrite pebbles and stones to the area which is now Chinese Turkestan. Today there is little nephrite in this area, and what remains is not of good quality. However, as recently as the eighteenth century, during the reign of the emperor Qian Long (r. 1736–95), one particularly large boulder was discovered. It was more than seven feet high and weighed almost seven tons.

A Chinese character pronounced *yu* is sometimes understood by Westerners to indicate true jade. Actually, both nephrite and various other stones from indigenous sources that resembled nephrite were used to create jewelry and ornamental figures in early China. Outside the imperial court there was always a far larger supply of false jades (such as the serpentines and soapstones) in circulation. The false jades, according to one scholar, were not thought of as different minerals. Nephrite was simply considered a yu of superior quality and durability.

The character yu may be of some interest to admirers of the dog of Fo. It closely resembles another character with the same pronunciation which means "ruler" or "imperial," and which is often found on the foreheads of images of Chinese lamaist dog-lions. If the carving in question is of a jadelike material, sometimes the presence of this character is mistakenly interpreted as indicating true jade. Actually, it is to be found on figures of dog-lions fashioned of many materials, including ivory and bronze. Perhaps it should be noted that the short-haired Pekingese, or Chinese Pug, was considered particularly desirable when the wrinkles on his forehead formed the "prince mark," three horizontal wrinkles in combination with a vertical indentation crossing them. This resembled the auspicious character yu.

Pure nephrite (and also jadeite) is white. This color has always been favored in China. The presence of other minerals, such as chromium, iron, and manganese, is responsible for the many hues in which jade may be found. Color was a matter of great significance in China. The basic elements of nature were

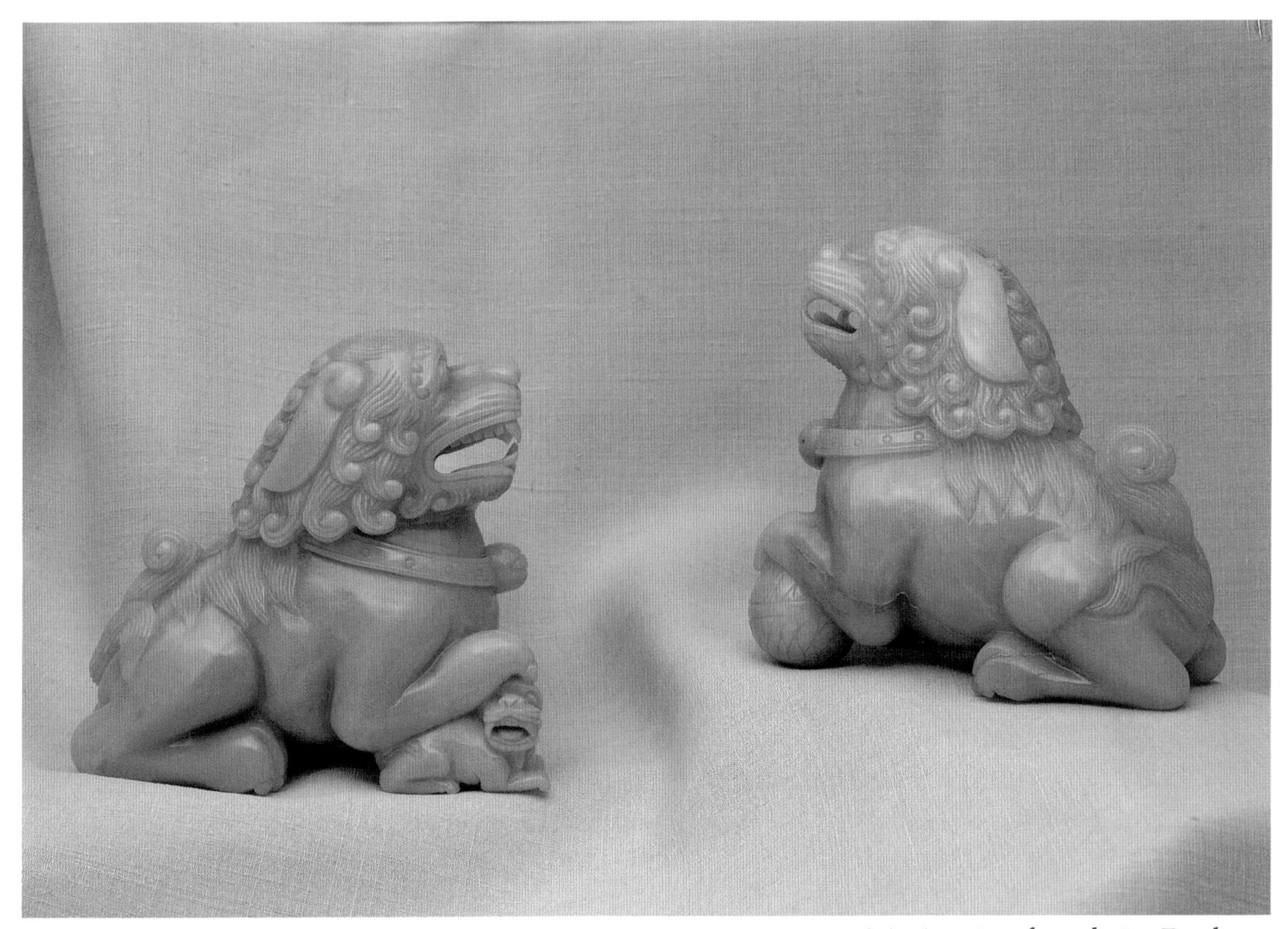

24. A pair of nephrite Fu dogs.

represented by yellow for earth, black for water, white for air, red for fire, and green for wood. The earth, heaven, and the four directions were also represented by distinguishing colors.

Some jade carvings incorporate more than one color. The second color may be from the crust or rind of the stone, but the occasional stone includes more than one hue. Such color combinations are picturesquely described as, for example, "moss entangled in snow." Other fanciful descriptions include "steamed chestnuts," "sky after rain," and "sky reflected in clear water."

Gump writes that nephrite was accorded a unique position in indigenous religion, "a place accorded no other substance. It was the link between earth and heaven. . . . In religious ceremonials the Emperor often used jade as we might a telephone, except that when he held up the jade Pi form [disc] and spoke through it he spoke to heaven. And through jade, Heaven was said to send its blessings in return."

In one way or another, jade was associated with all the major religions of China. Before the arrival of communism, Chinese Moslems were the miners, lapidaries, and merchants of nephrite. The stone was mined in predominantly Moslem territories. The lands along the Silk Road, which was the route taken by those who transported the uncut stone to China, were inhabited mainly by followers of Islam. Moslems, though devoted to the

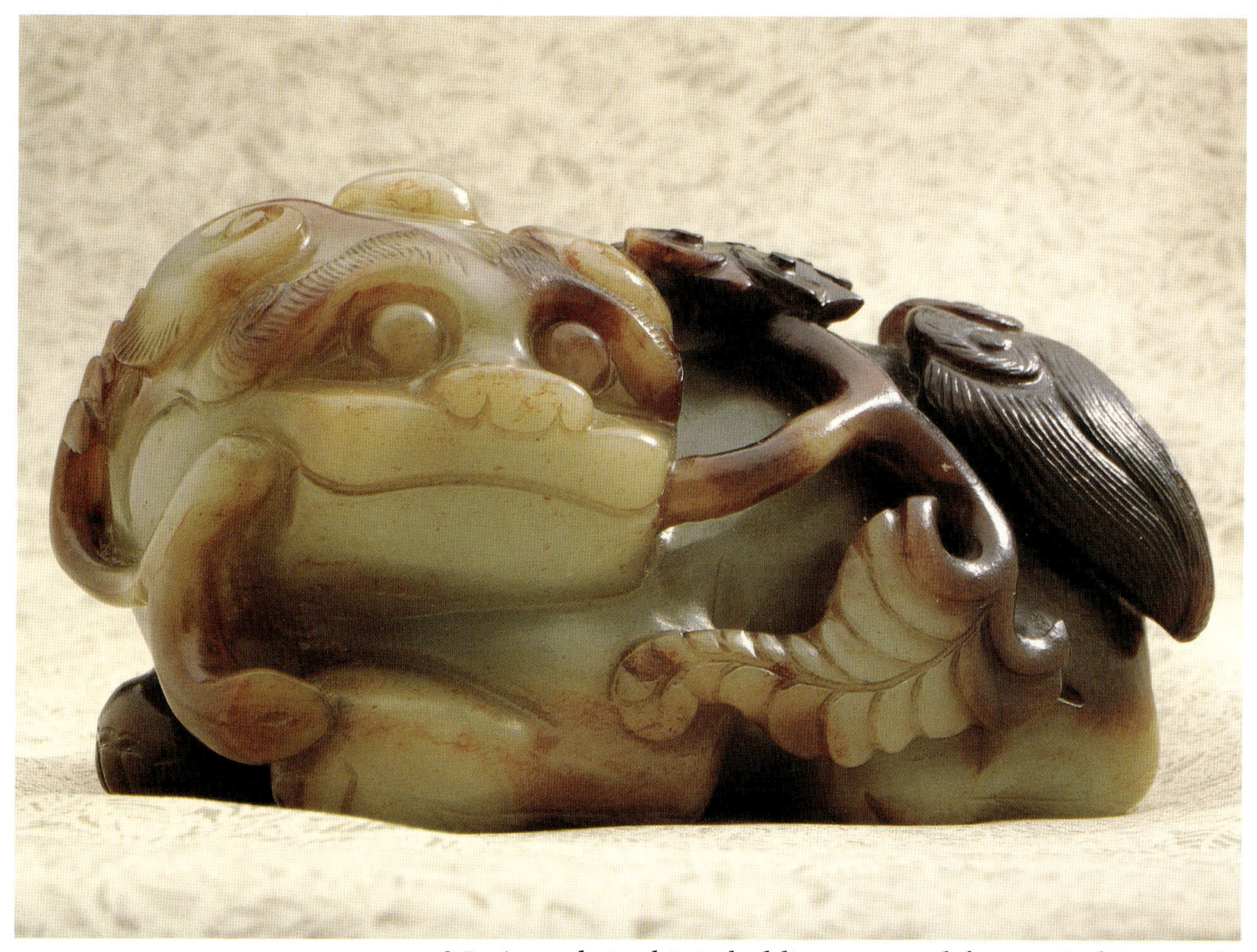

25. A nephrite bixie holding a sacred fungus in his mouth.

production and transportation of nephrite, created only vessels for their own preceremonial ablutions.

In the late seventeenth and early eighteenth centuries, Christian artifacts of worship were created of jade for the use of Chinese converts. However, a papal bull issued in 1742 required Chinese Catholics to renounce all aspects of Confucianism, ancestor worship, and belief in the Chinese heaven. This in turn inspired a revulsion in China against all things Christian and foreign and led to the persecution of Christians. During this period most Christian-inspired objects of jade, such as crucifixes, rosaries, and various church vessels, were destroyed or reworked into new forms.

Lao Zi, whose philosophy provided the foundation for what developed into the Daoist religion, is supposed to have advised his followers: "Do not wish to be rare like jade, or common like stone." This advice was overlooked by many Daoists, who believed that eternal life could be obtained by the consumption of a "pill of immortality," the magic elixir jade. Powdered jade was consumed in great quantities in this quest. It was also believed to provide a cure for all manner of complaints and to confer magical powers, including invisibility and levitation. In addition, jade provided protection against evil spirits and every misfortune.

Jade was also cherished by Chinese Buddhists, who treas-

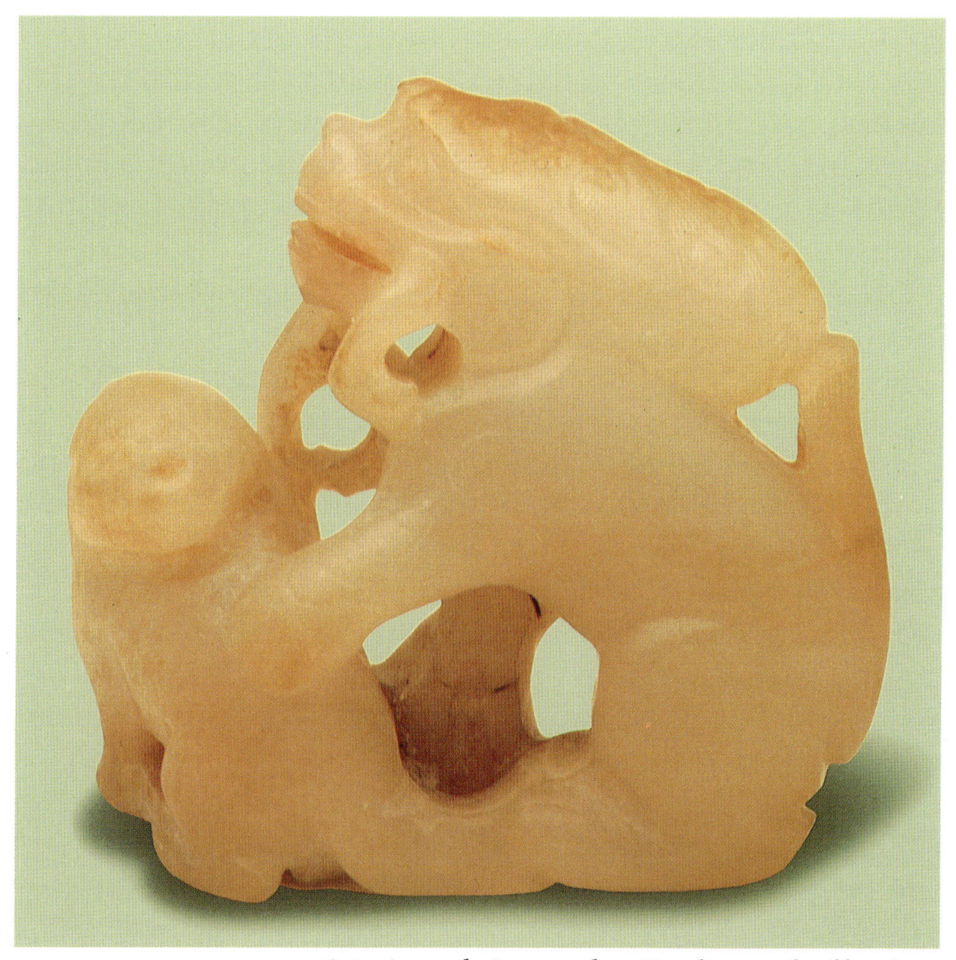

26. A nephrite mother Fu dog and offspring.

ured concrete symbols of their faith, as well as temple furnishings, made of mystical nephrite. Images of buddhas and bodhisattvas, meditation beads, incense burners, tablets of Buddhist scriptures, and tablets with scenes from the life of the Buddha or of one of the Buddhist heavens were among the creations of the nephrite worker.

Before the arrival of Buddhism in China, works of jade were usually small. Buddhist images, pagoda statues, and other artistic endeavors of Buddhist inspiration sometimes achieved impressive proportions. A five-foot Buddha and a nine-foot nephrite pagoda adorned with small brass bells are examples of this genre. Guanyin (Avalokitesvara in Sanskrit), the bodhisattva of compassion, protector of children and of all helpless creatures, has always been a favorite theme of the creator in jade.

The adherents of Chan (Zen in Japanese) Buddhism loved the spiritual dimension of nephrite, as did the Daoists and Confucianists. For the Chan disciple, jade was one way, one path, toward realization of the buddha-nature within man and all creation. A Chan master might give his disciple a small piece of nephrite on which to fix his concentration. This concentration can deepen into *samadhi,* the highest form of meditation. The subsequent realization of oneness with the stone as well as with all creation is what Chan disciples know as enlightenment.

Chinese jade artists were particularly adept at bird and animal carvings, rendering creatures both real and mythological. Some animal figures date back many centuries B.C. In those times, as in Chinese mythology, the boundaries between man and animal probably were not very clearly defined. Some historians believe that tribes or clans were represented by animals particularly admired for such qualities as courage, strength, or fleetness and that tribal totems evolved into heraldic symbols, as happened in other parts of the world.

A special class of animals related to the dog-lion was particularly favored by Chinese artists. Scholars have occasionally queried the possible reality of such beasts as the unicorn or the dragon. Could a creature with a horn in the center of his forehead once have existed? Could the dragon have been inspired by a giant alligator or lizard whose presence was most frequent after heavy rains and floods? Whatever the source of these strange beings, artists throughout East Asia found them a continuing source of inspiration. Many of the most interesting and beautiful works of jade, now the property of museums and private collectors worldwide, depict these strange and wonderful animals.

In the West, the dragon was a symbol of evil. Western mythology is well populated with dragon kidnappers of young girls, fire-breathing monsters who terrorized the helpless until liberation arrived in the form of a pure-hearted and courageous knight. In Asia, however, the dragon was a symbol of imperial sovereignty and the embodiment of wisdom and courage. He delivered proclamations, prophecies, and imperial edicts. Dragons were also associated with rain. Painted dragons were believed to come to life, producing storms with lightning and thunder.

As one Japanese writer explains, "The Eastern dragon is not the gruesome monster of medieval imagination, but the genius of strength and goodness. He is the spirit of change, therefore of life itself. We associate him with the supreme power or that sovereign cause which pervades everything, taking new forms according to its surroundings, yet never seen in a final shape. The dragon is the great mystery itself. Hidden in the caverns of inaccessible mountains, or coiled in the unfathomed depth of the sea, he awaits the time when he slowly rouses himself into activity. He unfolds himself in the storm clouds; he washes his mane in the blackness of the seething whirlpools. His claws are in the fork of the lightning, his scales begin to glisten in the bark of rain-swept pine-trees. His voice is heard in the hurricane which, scattering the withered leaves of the forest, quickens a new spring. The dragon reveals himself only to vanish."

It is impossible to think about the history of Chinese design without considering the myriad appearances of the dragon in ev-

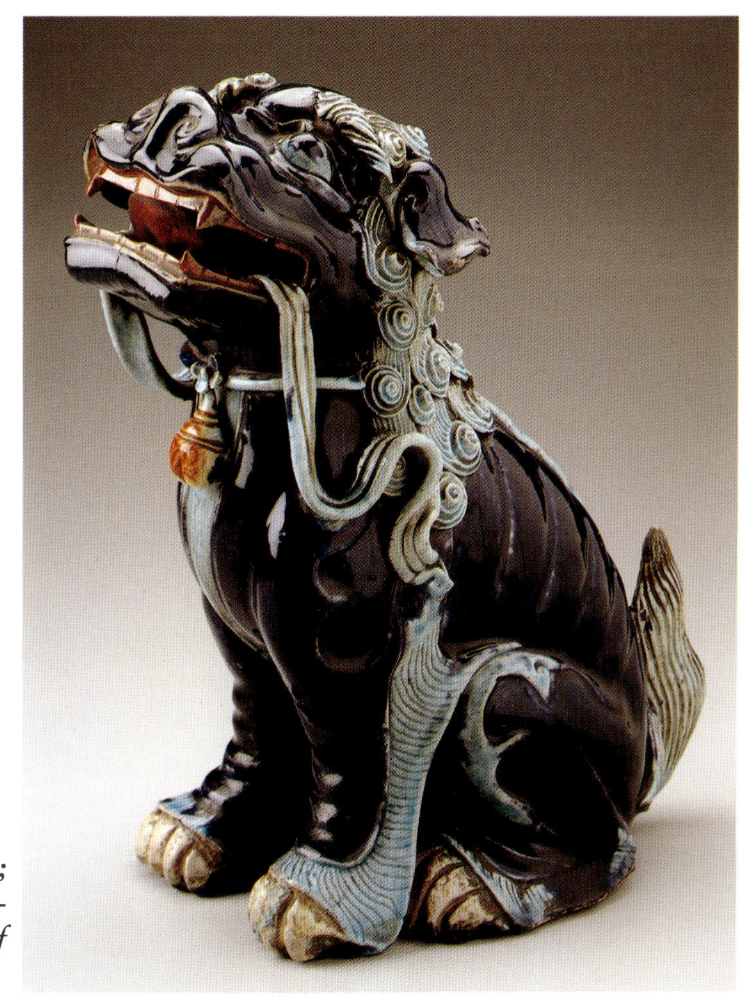

27. *A Chinese stoneware dog-lion; sixteenth century* A.D. *Courtesy, Museum of Fine Arts, Boston; gift of Mrs. F. G. Macomber.*

ery imaginable stone, metal, and textile. Dragons twine themselves around vases, urns, incense burners, and porcelain garden seats. They form handles for all manner of containers of metal and porcelain. They were embroidered with fine silk thread into elaborate designs for the garments of courtiers and emperors.

The dragon, the embodiment of the male, or yang, spirit, dwells among the clouds in the heavens. His close relative, the hydra, is distinguished by a double tail. He is a water dweller and holds dominion over rivers and oceans. Small, flat pieces of jade on which were incised dragon designs were thrown to him to ensure safe passage. "Dragon bones," unearthed by farmers plowing their fields, were in great demand as medicine. These bones were actually oracle bones from the Shang dynasty (ca. 1751–1123 B.C.) which had been used for divination. They were sold by Chinese apothecaries right through the nineteenth century.

A very Buddhist spirit is the Chinese unicorn, the *qilin* (*qi* means "male," and *lin* "female"). Its tread is so light that no insect, not even a blade of grass, can be injured under its hooves. Benevolence and gentleness towards all other creatures are the distinguishing traits of the qilin, who is believed to combine the best qualities of all furry animals. A composite creature, the qilin is supposed to have the head of a dragon, though it is often rather canine in appearance. A horn lies against the back of its head. It has the body of a deer, the hooves and legs of a pony, and the tail of a Shih Tzu. Other idiosyncracies include skin of five colors, a voice likened to the ringing of bells, and the ability to walk on water.

The Chinese unicorn is born from the conjunction of two stars and is seen on earth only at the time of the birth or death of a great man. It is the bearer of revelations and is believed to be the incarnate essence of the five elements. This legendary beast is supposed to live for a thousand years and is a solitary being. Buddhist artists have traditionally portrayed the qilin as carrying on its back the Tripitaka, the scrolls of the Buddhist canon.

The qilin was a great favorite of artists working in jade and first appeared in this medium during the Han dynasty (206 B.C.– A.D. 220). Usually depicted recumbent, it is one of the most appealing of the mythological animals, and its execution in pale translucent jade is appropriately otherworldly.

A mythical animal often difficult to distinguish from the dog-lion is the *bixie,* sometimes called the chimera. A bixie has the power to ward off evil spirits, as is indicated by the meaning of the two Chinese characters with which his name is written: *bi,* "to ward off," and *xie,* "evil spirit." The bixie also resembles the qilin and, like the qilin, is a composite creature. In Greek mythology the chimera was part serpent, part lion, and part goat. The bixie is predominantly leonine, with short legs, heavy paws, and a thick neck. His tail is elegantly curled and sometimes is noticeably serpentine, as is the ridged back found on later figures. His only goatlike attribute is his horn (or horns), which usually lies flat on the back of his head.

The bixies created in stone as giant guardians of the royal tombs of the so-called southern dynasties (420–589) are a massive embodiment of steadfast protection and majestic equanimity. Their large heads arch backward, their mouths are open (legend tells us bixies breath fire), and they gaze heavenward through the centuries. The tomb guardians are decorated with the suggestion of wings on their sides, though many bixies of later periods are unwinged. Some later bixies are very similar to the qilin, the legs and paws being the distinguishing features: the qilin may have a leonine head, but its hooves identify it as a unicorn.

An interesting jade incense burner/perfume container in the Imperial Palace Museum in Beijing is in the form of a variant of the horned, leonine bixie. This bixie has an odd, almost square form. He has a removable head and is hollow inside. Fumes from incense or perfume placed in the body were emitted through the beast's open mouth. Incense was believed to be a

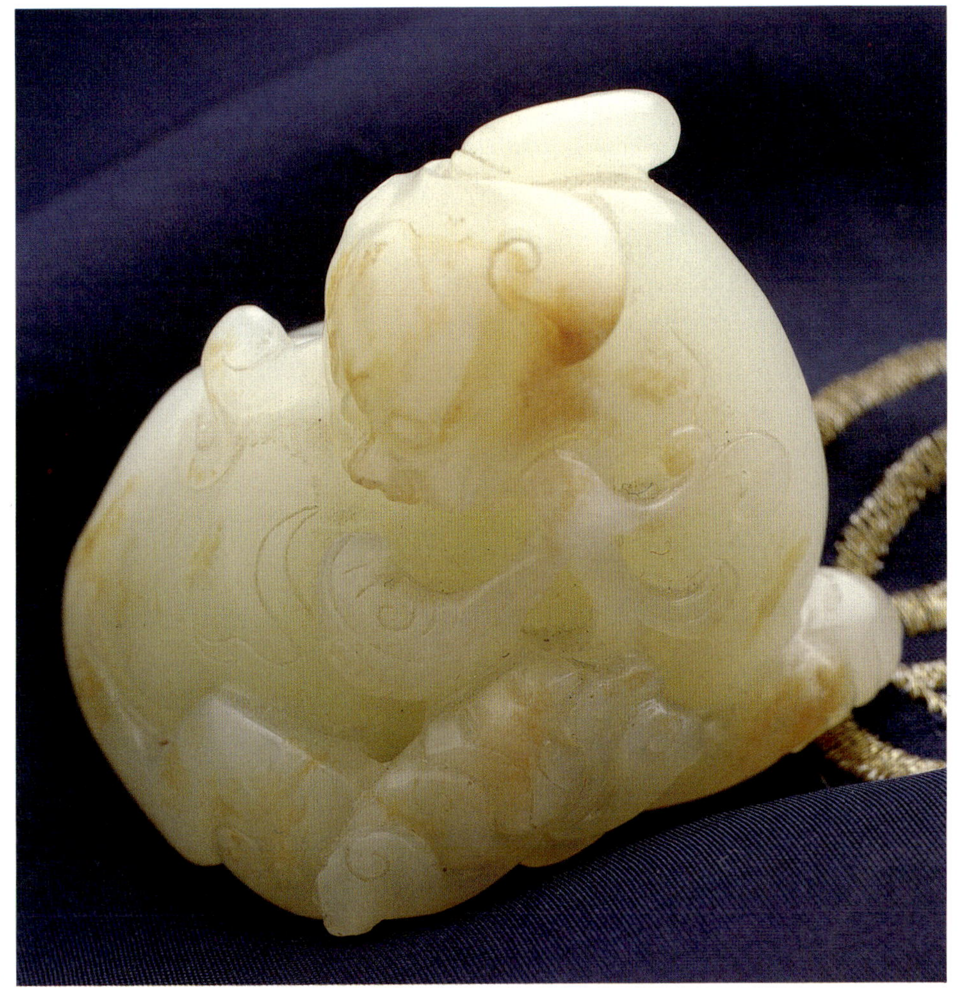

28. *A nephrite bixie.*

powerful protection against evil spirits. This white and light bluish-green jade bixie is mottled with the rusty hue of the jade crust. His forelegs are incised with dragon designs, while his hind legs are embellished with carved phoenixes.

Through these descriptions of a few of the mythological animals of China, the reader has observed the fluid nature of the otherworldly. The Chinese felt at home in all possible worlds. Nature, despite its changing moods, was not a force to be challenged or domesticated; rather, it was to be placated and lived with peaceably. Its myriad forms, in an eternal state of transformation, were a source of inspiration rather than apprehension or mistrust. Thus, celestial creatures exchanged features and attributes, displaying a remarkable variety through the centuries.

Scholars faced with a bevy of strange beasts to identify for a catalogue or other scholarly enterprise are often reduced to labeling them "mythical animals," "feline chimeras," "feline-looking unicorns," "doglike monsters," "single-horn animals," or "winged animals." Chimeras and lions were frequently equipped with wings. In the Ming dynasty (1368–1644) they were sometimes depicted riding on clouds, occasionally carrying flowers (usually peonies), acanthus leaves, or the *lingzhi* (sacred fungus) in their mouths. Both lions and unicorns had doglike faces, with varying degrees of similarity to the dog-lion. All these animal spirits were embodied in many metals and stones. Those created in jade were special treasures, uniting a bit of heaven and a bit of earth for their fortunate human owners. According to poetic Chinese sentiment, "the propitious air of heaven and earth is always condensing into jade."

As with all jade creations, the finest of dog-lion carvings were not superimposed on "the stone of heaven." As Gump so truly observes, it was the gift of the true jade artist to discover the cosmic creature within the material and then to reveal it.

THE SHISHI AND THE ART OF THE JAPANESE NETSUKE

The high point in Chinese history for the Shih Tzu, as for their cousins the Pekingese, was at the Manchu court. There eunuchs vied in their efforts to oversee the development of handsome, furry replicas of the mount of Manjusri Bodhisattva. As companions for aristocrats and monks, lion-dogs flourished and were cherished and well cared for. Flat-faced dogs were not among the creatures sentenced to the cooking pot even in times of want or social upheaval. Their lives were passed in luxurious surroundings, and few humans thought of them as "only dogs." It could not have occurred to those fortunate Buddhist creatures

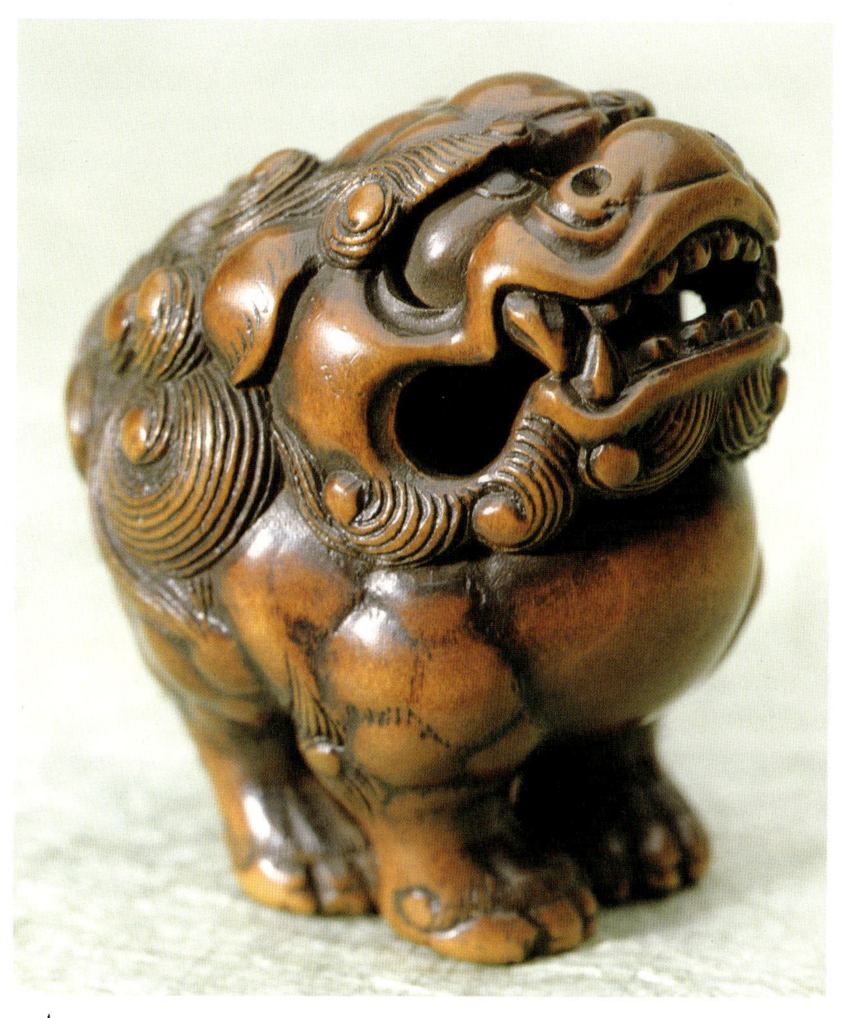

29. *A wood netsuke of a shi-shi in the form of an incense burner.*

to think of themselves in that way, either. Unlike many Chinese, the Japanese were fond of dogs and valued them as dependable and loyal friends. In Japan the lion-dog's near relative, the Japanese Chin, was cultivated in imperial circles, though never on the scale of the Manchu court's cultivation of its lion-dog.

The dog-lion, or *shishi*, of Japanese art and legend was also known as the Buddhist temple dog. Swept along in the great cultural stream that made its way from China through Korea to Japan, the dog of Fo was to lose some of his imperial functions while living among the people of Japan. Formally seated creatures in pairs are rarely seen in Japan, except before some Buddhist altars and tombs. Although some aspects of lamaist Buddhism are also found in the Japanese Shingon sect, this form of Buddhist teaching did not popularize Manjusri Bodhisattva and his shishi companion. With the development of the Zen sect in the thirteenth century, however, Manjusri seated on his celestial shishi appeared in meditation halls in Zen temples.

Perhaps the Japanese were persuaded that the shishi should not spend eternity guarding sacred buildings. Rather, he should submit to the Buddhist doctrine of constant change and becoming, as can be seen from the following tale. Two shishi, quite devoted to each other, who had spent centuries in peaceful immobility before a Japanese temple, one day engaged in a dispute.

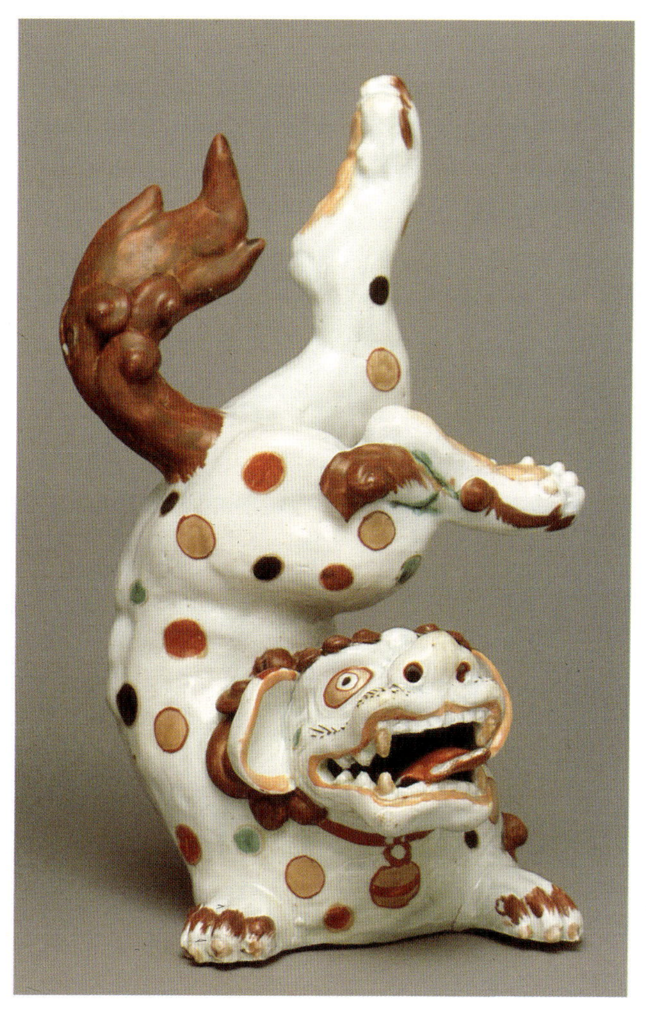

30. *An ebullient Arita-ware shishi.*

The disagreement became heated, and the two creatures leapt from their pedestals to the ground. The descent was too much for them, and they shattered into a thousand pieces.

Happily, the dog-lion was to find a new and prolific incarnation in the Edo period. The art of the *netsuke,* or ornamental toggle, was cultivated by craftsmen and sculptors in this time when Japan was largely isolated from foreign influences. No longer was the sculpted dog of Buddha required to remain immobilized before altars or to provide transport for the fierce bodhisattva of wisdom.

The netsuke is an ornament designed to attach various appendages to the obi, or kimono sash. The toggle contains a hole (*himotoshi*), artfully integrated into the design of the sculpture, through which is passed a silk cord. From the end of this cord may be suspended a brush case, a pipe, seals, keys, or a tiered lacquer container (*inro*) for tobacco or medicinal herbs. The toggle is secured on the top edge of the obi, and the suspended object is held in place on the cord by a carved bead (*ojime*). The kimono, designed without pockets, allows the wearer no other means to carry about the many small necessities of life.

Netsuke, miniature sculptures, are infused with a sense of light-hearted irony. They are to conventional sculpture what the satirical *senryu* verse of Edo-period Japan was to the haiku or

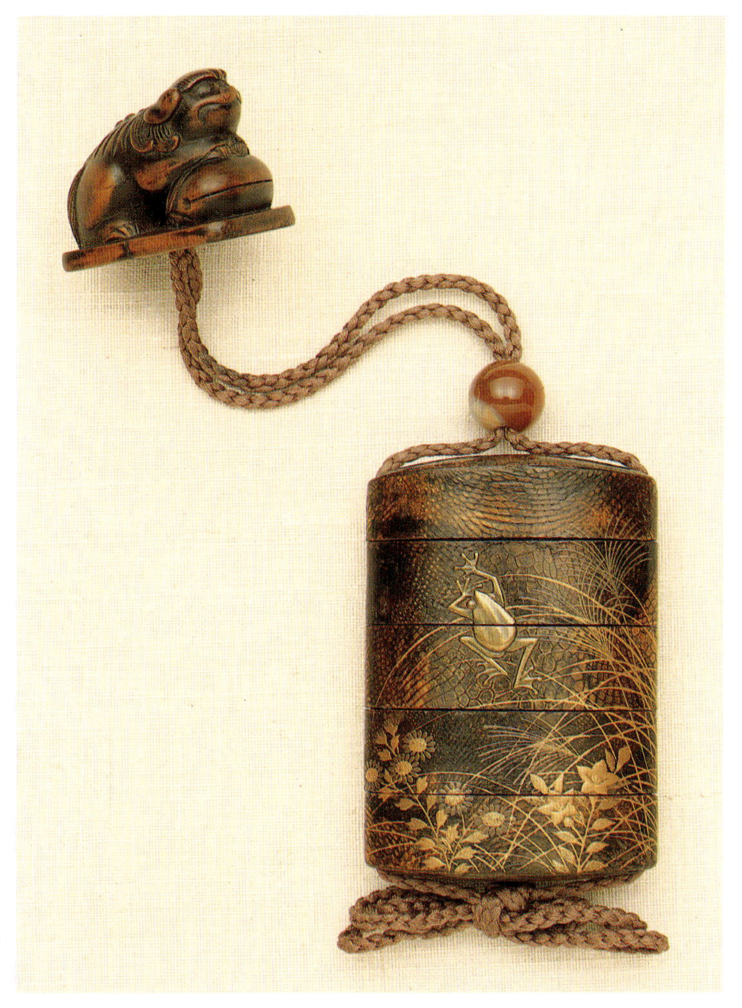

31. *An inro with a wood netsuke in the form of a shishi.*

the *waka*. In an authoritarian society where social and literary forms were strictly dictated, full expression of satire and fantasy was permitted to the senryu writer and the netsuke carver. These two art forms are thus a source of many interesting insights into Japanese life and mentality.

Originally inspired by the jade and stone dogs of Fo from China, cavorting with their balls and bows, peonies and acanthus leaves, Japanese netsuke carvers produced great numbers of the tiny creatures in an infinite variety of spirited forms. The shishi is seen emerging from an egg, concealed inside a vegetable, or standing on his head on top of a ball. He may be encased in a hollow sphere composed of peony flowers and foliage. In both China and Japan the peony was considered the king of flowers and was properly associated with the shishi, the king of beasts.

More realistically, artists brought forth from their materials shishi lying on their backs scratching themselves and paternal dog-lions watching over both a cub and a ball, the latter often containing a bead symbolizing the jewel (*tama*) of the Buddhist teaching. Shishi wrestling with other shishi, pursuing tigers or bears, lying on their backs playing with the tama they are supposed to be guarding, or being carried about lovingly by smiling Daoist hermits (*sennin*) are among the many creations of netsuke carvers.

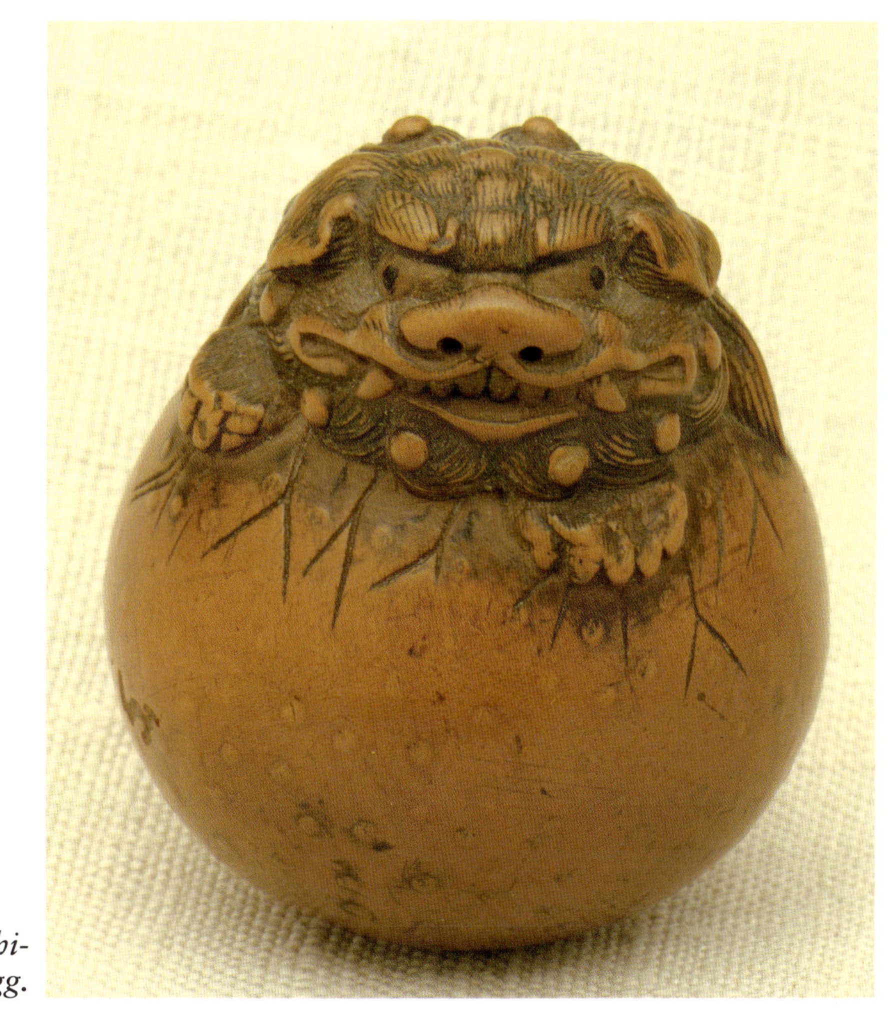

32. *A wood netsuke of a shi-shi being born from an egg.*

The first netsuke were made from stones, gourds, or walnut shells. Doughnut-shaped rings were probably among the earliest forms. Small sculptures carved on all sides, including the bottom, were probably not in use before the eighteenth century. Chinese influence on all the arts of Japan suggests that the jade toggles of China may have inspired the earliest Japanese netsuke. But whatever influences may have been at work, the netsuke is essentially and uniquely Japanese. Living in a small mountainous country, the Japanese became wonderfully adept at making the most of limited spaces and cultivating miniaturization in all forms, from gardens to sculpture.

The intricately carved netsuke originated as articles of everyday use. Today, in auction rooms all over the world, thousands of dollars are paid for the finest examples. Though modern imitations of eighteenth- and nineteenth-century pieces are a cottage industry in Hong Kong, to the trained eye they cannot match the artistry and charm of authentic carvings. The creation of beautiful things for the most mundane functions was an expression of the reverence held by traditional Japanese for life in all its forms. And the spirit of the dog-lion has never been more ebulliently embodied than in the netsuke.

Japan's temperate climate, generous rainfall, and appropriate soil conditions combined to provide the carver with a great

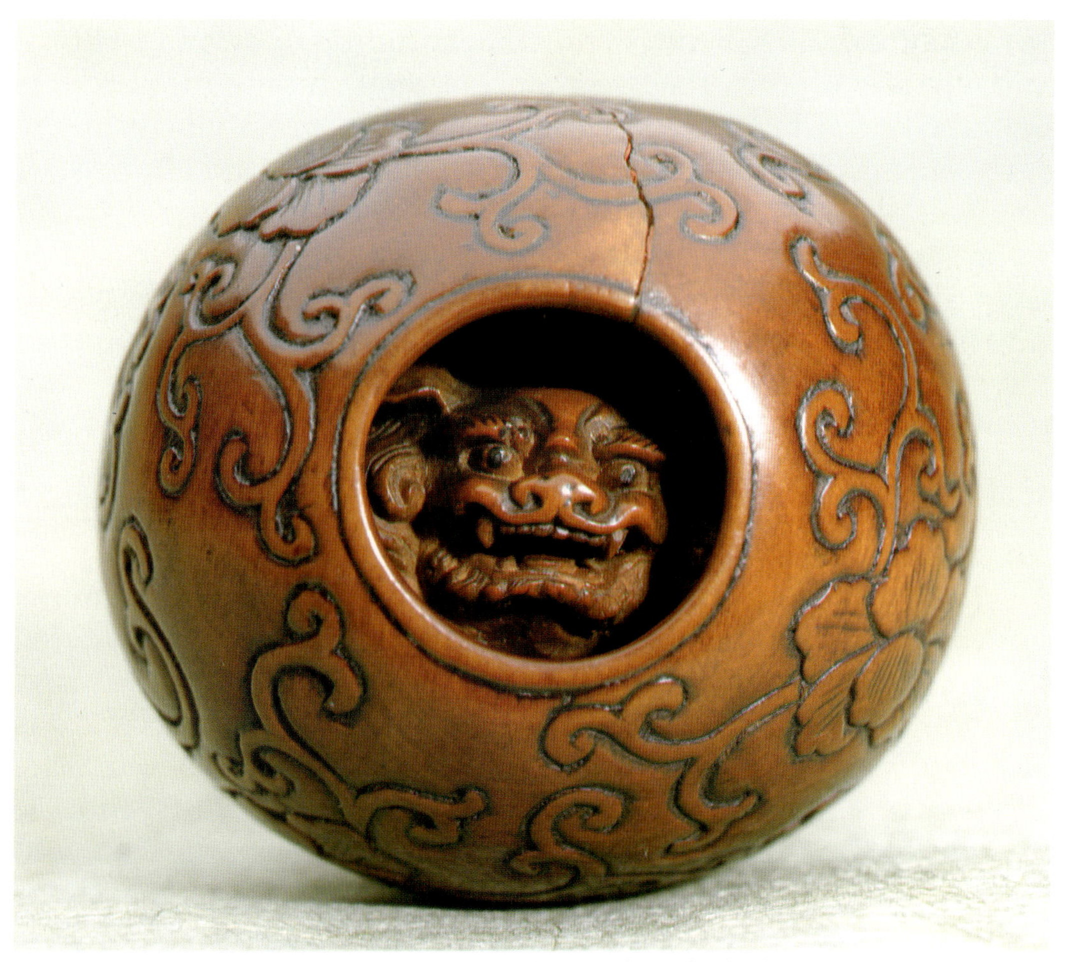

33. A wood netsuke of a ball containing a shishi.

variety of woods. Cherry, cypress, persimmon, yew, pine, ebony, and boxwood were the most appreciated, with boxwood the material most favored by netsuke carvers, particularly in the early nineteenth century. The patina, fine grain, and strength of this pale, hard wood make it ideal for woodcarving. Age and wear improve its luster, and it is extremely durable. Netsuke were also made from camphorwood, jujube, and sandalwood. The finished carving was polished with a horsehair brush and an old silk cloth. The natural oil from the skin of the carver's hand provided the only finish necessary. Essential to a fine netsuke, according to Barbra Okada, is the untranslatable quality of *aji:* a netsuke possessing aji is infused with the spirit of the carver, and this is communicated by the feel as well as the look of the toggle.

Jade was a link between heaven and earth for the Chinese. For the Japanese, wood provided a special bond with the sacred "emptiness." If "the propitious air of heaven and earth is always condensing into jade" for the continuing edification of Chinese sensibilities, that same propitious air may be said to penetrate the soil of Japan, bringing forth other jewels: forests and orchards. The many sorts of wood that the Japanese cultivate and use so reverently and imaginatively provide the materials for houses, temples, and shrines, as well as for sculpture and for lacquerware.

Japanese civilization is almost unimaginable without wood, bamboo, and rice. The depth of the Japanese feeling for wood may puzzle the reader. The choice of wood as a special link with eternity, rather than a harder, rarer substance, may seem surprising. Some Westerners may prefer a diamond, or even a plebeian "rock of ages," to the softer, more vulnerable gift of the soil.

Eternity is found within all things, animate and inanimate, in traditional Japanese philosophy. The inspiration of the eternal is, according to this understanding, best experienced through a material which is visibly mutable. The apparent immutability of stone is less interesting to the Japanese imagination than a visible capacity for transformation. The sort of permanence that appeals to a traditional Japanese is to be found in an old temple that has been completely rebuilt, bit by bit, many times through the centuries. An entity in a constant state of change that survives the centuries, ever the same yet ever different, truly represents the jewel of the Buddha's Dharma. Eternity is not static. It is an endless process of transformation and becoming.

Wood has always been the preferred material of the creators of great sculpture in Japan. Furthermore, according to one scholar of Japanese Buddhist art, "When ninth century esoteric Buddhist sculptors began to leave unpainted the surfaces of solid wooden images, they were in part reflecting the Shinto belief that because the sacred resides in natural elements such as trees, the material should be left in as natural a form as possible."

Otherworldly buddhas and remarkably realistic carvings of human followers were creations of the artist in wood. Among the creators of wood images of buddhas and ascetics were carvers of netsuke. In the seventeenth century small Buddhist altars for use in homes became popular. The *butsudan* (buddha shelf) was a shrine containing a Buddhist image and special miniature tablets bearing the names of departed family members. The craftsmen who worked on the furnishings for the butsudan also turned a hand to netsuke. Netsuke were carved first by artisans who did not sign their work, and later by artists whose names were to become known worldwide to museum curators and collectors.

Since this is the tale of the lion-dog, the reader can be given only a brief suggestion of the scope of the subject matter and materials of netsuke. Figures mythological and human, Oriental and Occidental, flowers, vegetables, birds, and insects, as well as animals mundane and legendary, were all dealt with, often in a whimsical and sardonic spirit. One curious and ingenious theme was "the dream of the clam." The partially open clam shell reveals the scene of an underwater palace. Subjects popular in the nineteenth century included insect, animal, and vegetable group-

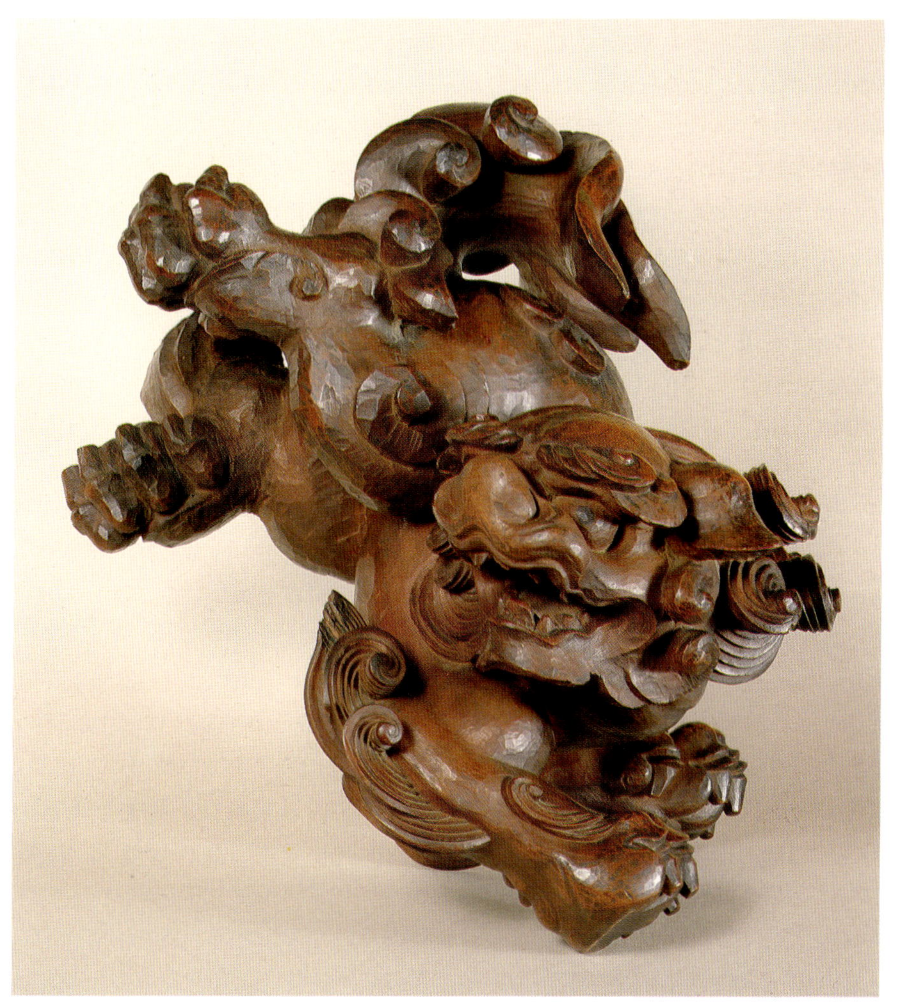

34. *A spirited wood shi-shi, probably a temple ornament.*

ings, a naked woman standing in a wooden tub scratching herself, an octopus reading a "pillow book" (a kind of illustrated sex manual intended for brides), and a pavilion containing figures in Chinese dress playing chess.

Though wood was highly favored by netsuke artists, the number of materials used at one time or another by the makers of toggles is almost infinite. Lacquer, ivory, horn, bamboo, malachite, coral, amber, goldstone, and porcelain netsuke are sometimes seen. Metals, such as alloys of copper and silver or copper and gold, are relatively common. Less usual are toggles of silver or gold. Many of these materials were used to make eyes for wood animal netsuke or to gild special pieces. Ebony inlay as well as ivory hands and faces are found on the occasional piece. For the lover of simple, rustic things, there are carvings made from nuts and apricot or peach stones.

One of the earliest types of netsuke was the shishi, known to have been about in the seventeenth century. Seventeenth- and eighteenth-century netsuke are usually in the form of legendary or mythological figures carved with vitality and originality. Human figures are occasionally six or seven inches high, and animals are more than an inch in height. They are more fancifully conceived than nineteenth-century figures, which are more realistic. From the early period come strong, impish shishi with vivid

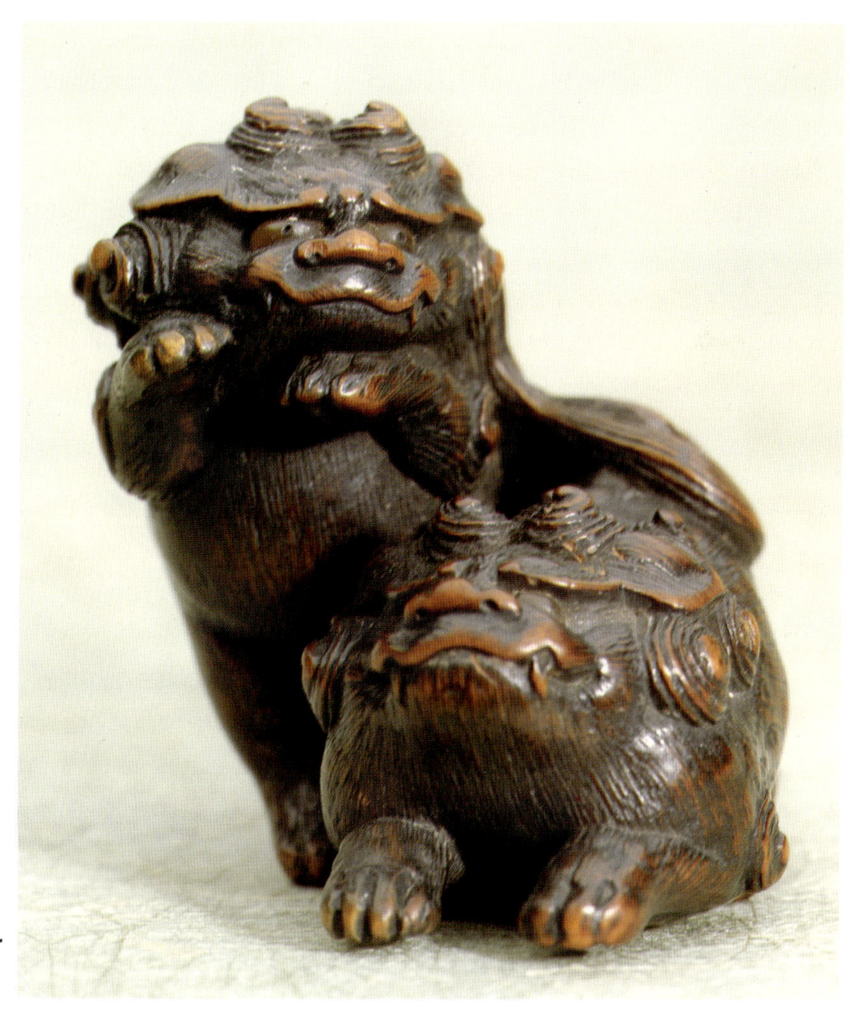

35. *A wood netsuke of a pair of shishi.*

expressions, interestingly mottled backs, and profuse, voluted manes and tails. In the nineteenth century smaller and more intricately carved creatures with delicate detail were popular. For example, the shishi's openwork ball often contains a small bead within, visible through the openings. This curious detail represents an interesting feat, since the shishi was almost always carved from one block of wood, and the bead, also part of the block, was carved inside the outer sphere. This bead is the jewel which symbolizes the Buddhist teaching.

Of the main types of netsuke, most common are the figures worked in *katabori*. These are small solid sculptures carved on all surfaces, including the bottom. Another type of netsuke is a simple bowl-shaped carving with a lid or cover, often made of metal. The silk cord which makes the netsuke fast to the obi tightens or releases the lid. The lid may be worked in relief or inlaid with other materials. Because of its shape, this form is named for a bean cake, the *manju,* which the Japanese enjoy on special festive occasions. The little containers are usually flat and circular. Occasionally the manju is square or oval, however, and sometimes it is not a container but a solid form decorated in relief.

The *ryusa* netsuke is a creation which requires considerable skill, particularly when executed in one piece. This form of ne-

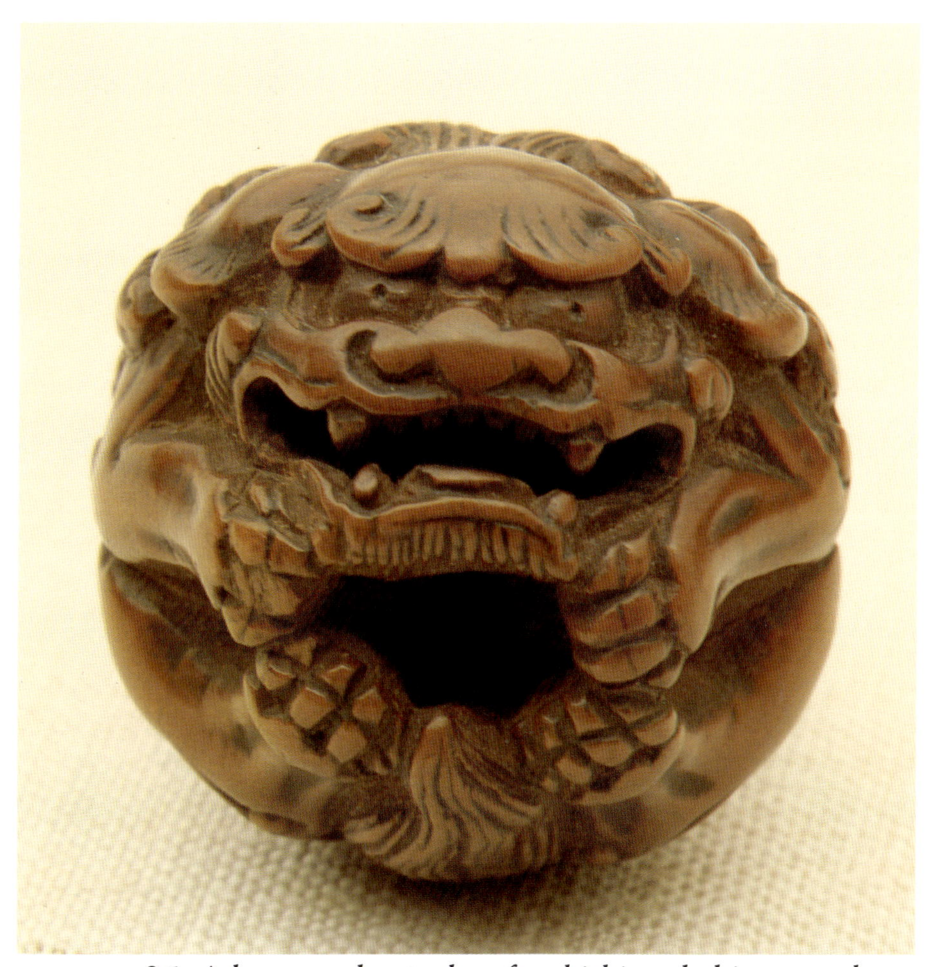

36. A boxwood netsuke of a shishi curled into a sphere.

tsuke takes its name from an eighteenth-century carver. His specialty was a hollow ball whose surface was usually carved with a variety of still-life forms. Often these consisted of an elaborate tangle of flowers or other vegetation. One example of a ryusa shishi is a round feline-looking creature with all four feet tucked together at the bottom and his head lowered to create a spherical shape. The ryusa is very lightweight and delicate. It probably would not have been a very practical addition to a person's wardrobe, particularly if it was expected to support a heavy object, such as a lacquer inro and its contents.

A netsuke very popular with admirers of Japanese *bugaku* dance is the miniature mask. Bugaku was taken to Japan from the Tang court in the eighth century. The masks, both human and animal, are sometimes grotesque. They may portray ugly or unfortunate people with warped features or sorrowful expressions. The bird and animal masks are often ferocious. Originally the netsuke masks were made by the carvers of the larger originals worn on the stage. The miniature copies were later supplemented by contorted or comical variations of the original faces.

Another well-known dance mask is that of the shishi, which is worn during the performance of the *shishi-mai,* or "lion dance." The lion dance was performed first in China and was known there as "exercising the lions." It is a New Year's dance.

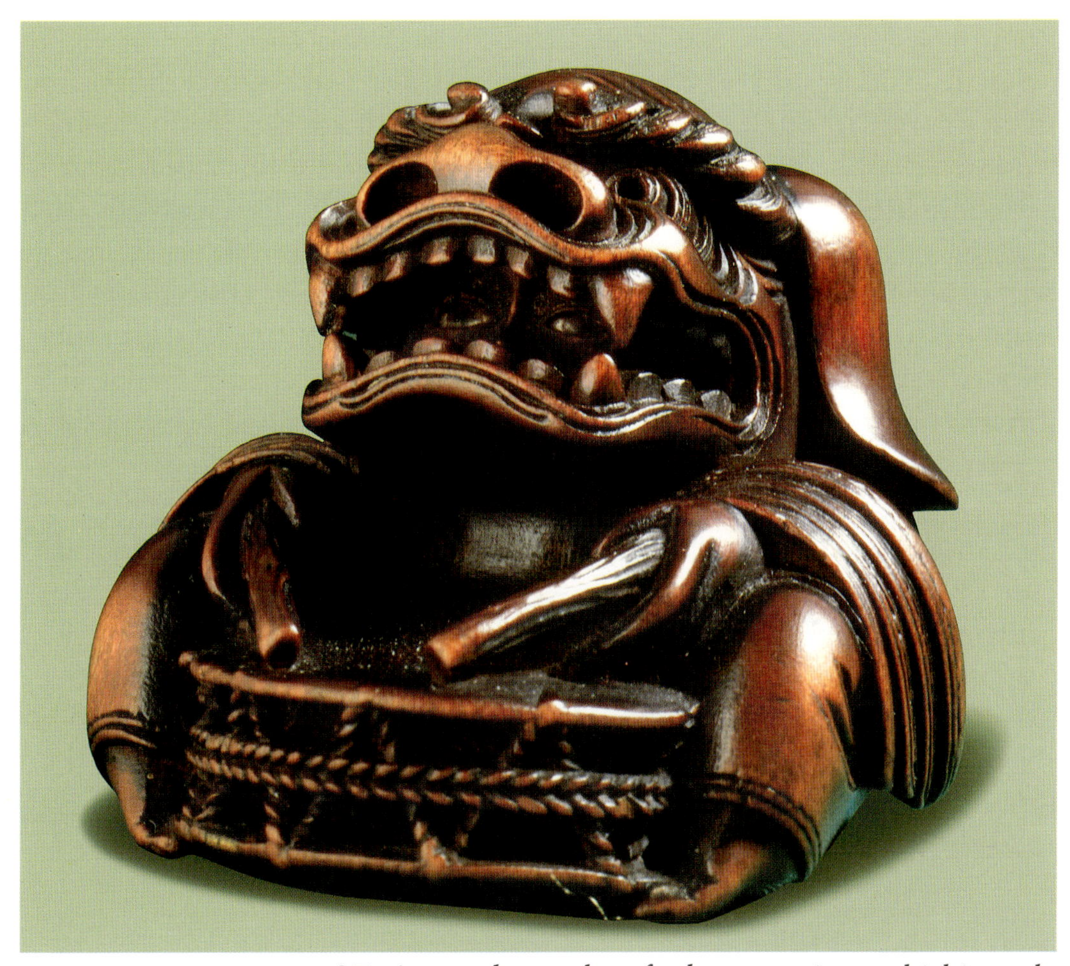

37. A wood netsuke of a boy wearing a shishi mask.

A man or boy wears the large lion's-head mask. A second person operates the front end of the lion costume, and a third is clothed in the rear end of the beast's costume. In China the lion is sent in pursuit of a large colorful ball. In Japan the dance was incorporated into bugaku performances. There is a legendary tale of a dancer who performed the lion dance with such passionate intensity that he was possessed by the lion's spirit and finally became a lion. It is sometimes observed that the Shih Tzu falls into a distinctive gait that is not unlike that of the creature of the lion dance. Particularly when he is obliged to run on wet grass, his rocking motion is reminiscent of that of the shishi-mai.

The woodcarvers of Japan, like the workers in jade of China, greatly fancied mythological creatures. Much of the subject matter for sculpture was inspired by pictures, and a book entitled the *Ressenden* was the source of knowledge of mythological beasts. To modern Western taste, some of these creatures are figments of nightmare, visions of a disordered realm. However, if realistic and rational expectations are set aside, they emerge as an interesting dimension of the mythological fancy, rooted in a deep and primitive layer of the psyche.

Among these strange creations is an animal called the *baku*. The baku has the short, heavy body, paws, mane, and tail of a shishi and the head of an elephant. In the finest eighteenth-

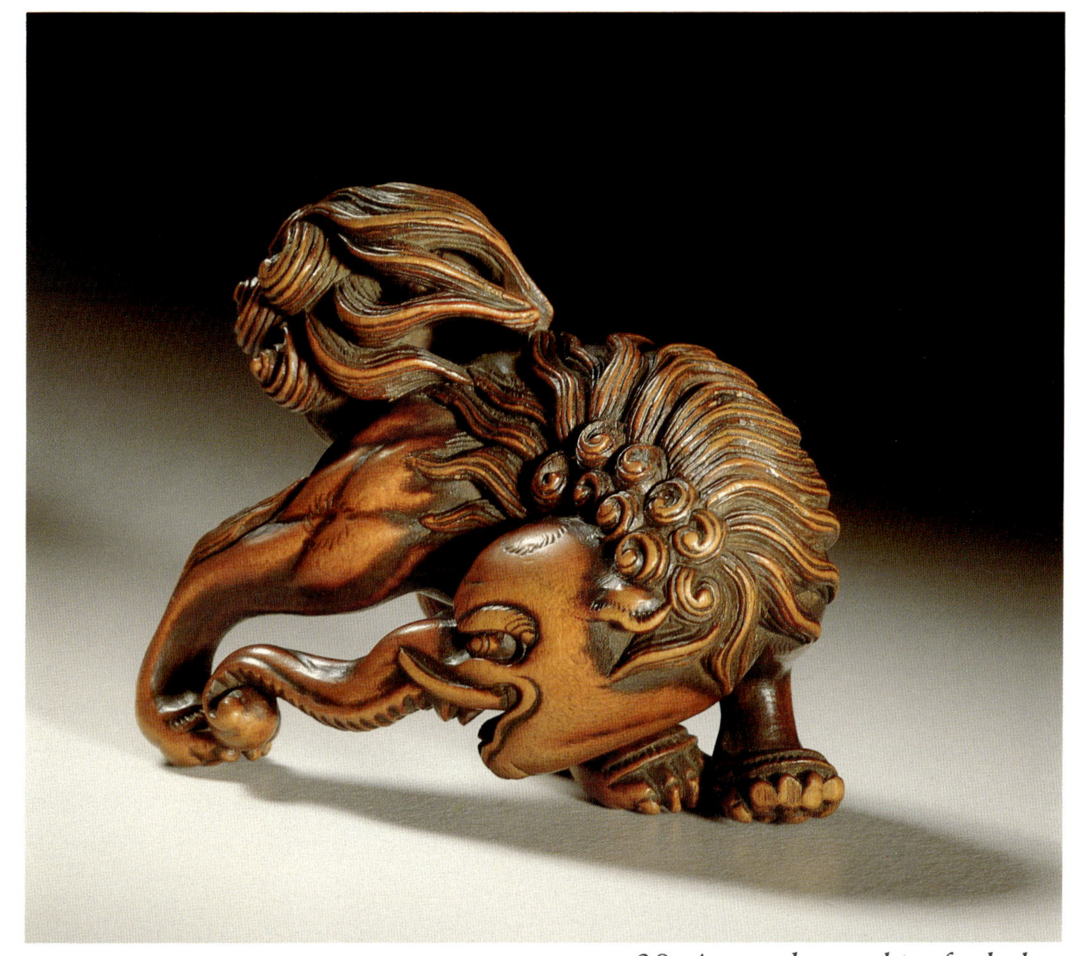

38. A wood netsuke of a baku.

century netsuke, this creature is covered with elaborate Buddha snail-curls. His body, like the bodies of some early shishi, is mottled with circular protuberances indicating vigorous muscles. Once, according to legend, the baku spoke with a human voice. However, his most important quality from the human point of view is his appetite for bad dreams. When caught in the throes of a nightmare, the dreamer calls out three times, "Eat it, baku!" The obliging creature devours the unpleasant dream on the spot. The Chinese character for baku was once painted on headrests to promote peaceful, dreamless sleep. In netsuke art, the baku is occasionally shown playing with a headrest. The baku has one other function. The characters for "plainwood deity," another name for him, were painted on housefronts to protect the inhabitants against plague.

In Japan the Chinese unicorn, the qilin, is called the *kirin*. It is thought to have a dragon's head with a single horn, a deer's body, equine legs and hooves, and the tail of a shishi. It is a graceful creature with an abundance of snail-curls and a benevolent, dreamy expression. Its close relative, the *hakutaku,* resembles it in nearly every respect except for the head and feet. The hakutaku has a dog-lion's head and round leonine paws.

A group of composite animals who rarely appear as netsuke or even as larger sculptures in Japan includes the *kaiba,* the *sui-*

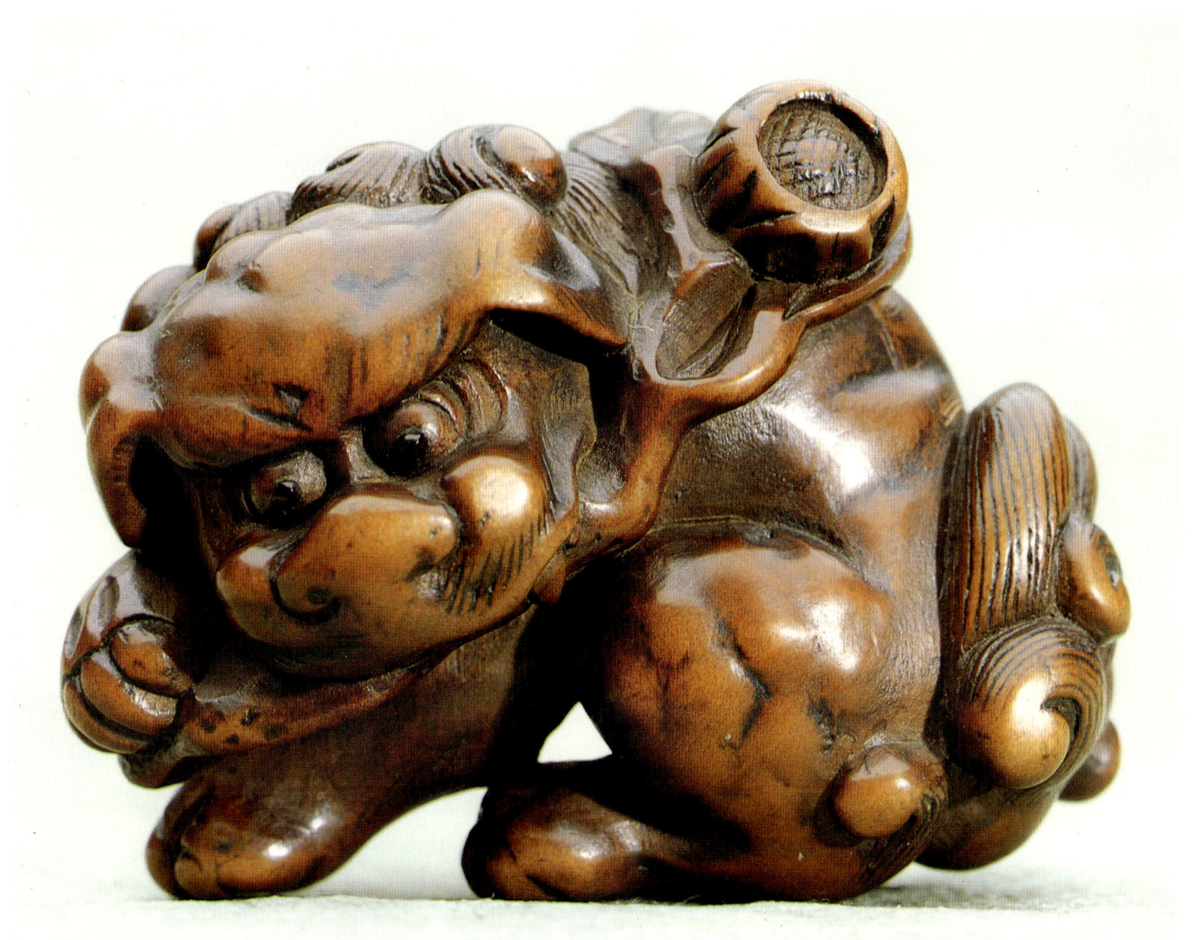

39. A wood netsuke of a shishi holding a peony in his mouth.

sei, the *kudan,* and the *nue.* The first of these creatures of legend, the kaiba, is a winged horse, an Oriental Pegasus. The suisei is a sort of rhinoceros with a carapaced back. Sometimes he has a single horn, sometimes two or even three. According to Paul Moss, "The sacred one-horned suisei cannot see its own shadow, and drinks from moving water so as not to have its own reflection in its eyes." The kudan is kin to the centaur. He has the body of a bull, a bearded human head, and an extra pair of eyes on each side of his body. Finally, there is the nue, who has a monkey's head, a badger's back, a dragon's scales, and a snake's tail.

With the possible exception of the winged horse, none of these animals has provided Oriental artists with the inspiration of the dog-lion, of the bixie, of the qilin or kirin, or of the baku. Perhaps these four appeared more sympathetic, not to mention more useful, to humans, as guardians, as helpers, or as harbingers of good times. All the composite beings of Oriental sculpture are, at least in part, symbols of the transience of things, of the unexpected and the unknown. Though feared, what is not understood has inspired an enduring fascination.

CHAPTER FIVE

LION-DOGS, SNOW-LIONS, AND THE ARTS OF TIBET

Tibet was the home of the Shih Tzu's Lhasa Apso ancestors as well as of their legendary counterpart, the snow-lion, who appears on the Tibetan flag and on the personal seal of the Dalai Lama. Therefore we will now examine a few aspects of this remote, little-known civilization, of Tibetan dogs, and of the snow-lion (dog-lion) symbol of Tibetan art.

Bounded by China to the north and east and by Nepal and India to the south, Tibet covers an area more than five times the size of England, Scotland, and Wales combined. In this country are the world's highest mountains, deep and dangerous gorges, swift-flowing rivers, and vast desert wastelands. Protracted winters bring violent, icy winds and heavy snow. Summers are hot and subject to dust-bearing wind storms. The capital city, Lhasa, is about twelve thousand feet above sea level, and until the late 1950s was the center of a colorful Buddhist culture. Above the valley floor, the cultivation of barley, corn, rice, and turnips, as well as some fruit and nut trees, is accomplished with difficulty because of the necessity for continual irrigation. A large part of the Tibetan population is made up of shepherds, often nomadic, who tend flocks of sheep, goats, asses, yaks, and dzo, a cross of cow and yak.

Among Tibetan Buddhists in Nepal, according to Corneille Jest, "la consommation de viande est occasionelle." A slaughter is a collective decision so that guilt can be shared. A man of the lowest class (*be-ra*) is assigned the onerous task of slaughter. Animals killed by accident are also eaten.

The canine being has a special friend in the Tibetan. In many non-Western countries, particularly in the Middle East, dogs are disliked and abused. They are outcast creatures. But Tibetans of all classes, whether prosperous urban merchants or tent-dwelling nomads, are dog lovers. In Tibetan communities dogs are never gastronomic candidates, and the dog-meat eaters of such countries as Korea and China are viewed with revulsion.

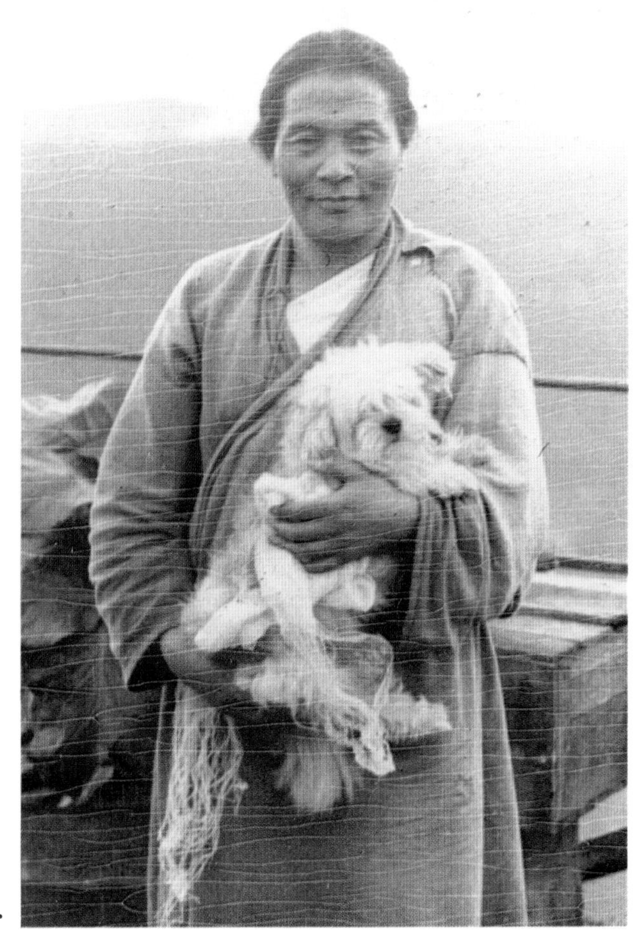

40. *A Tibetan lama holding a Lhasa Apso.*

Even dogs in nomadic encampments are given personal names. The respect in which they are held is indicated by the Buddhist names with which canine friends and protectors may be favored. Sangs rGyas (pronounced Sang-gye), which may be translated as "The Buddhahood," is an interesting example.

It was not the small lion-dog that was most common in old Tibet but the giant guard dog, or "door dog." Tibetan Mastiffs and large mongrels with some Mastiff blood were kept in great numbers in herding communities. Before the Chinese occupation of the country, a nomad family would usually have had at least two dogs; a rich chieftain might have had as many as twenty. These tent guardians fiercely watched over their families and their property. Off duty, the dogs were the special friends of the women, and the puppies were the children's playmates. Such were the regard and respect shown to watchdogs that there were certain restrictions on the measures humans could employ against these ferocious protectors. One could not use spear points, sharp-edged weapons, and firearms against a dog unless one was prepared to face the owner's wrath.

Three types of companion dogs known and loved in the West today were the mascots and the "sleeping dogs," the indoor companions of urban dwellers and monastics, in old Tibet: the Lhasa Apso, the Tibetan Terrier, and the Tibetan Spaniel.

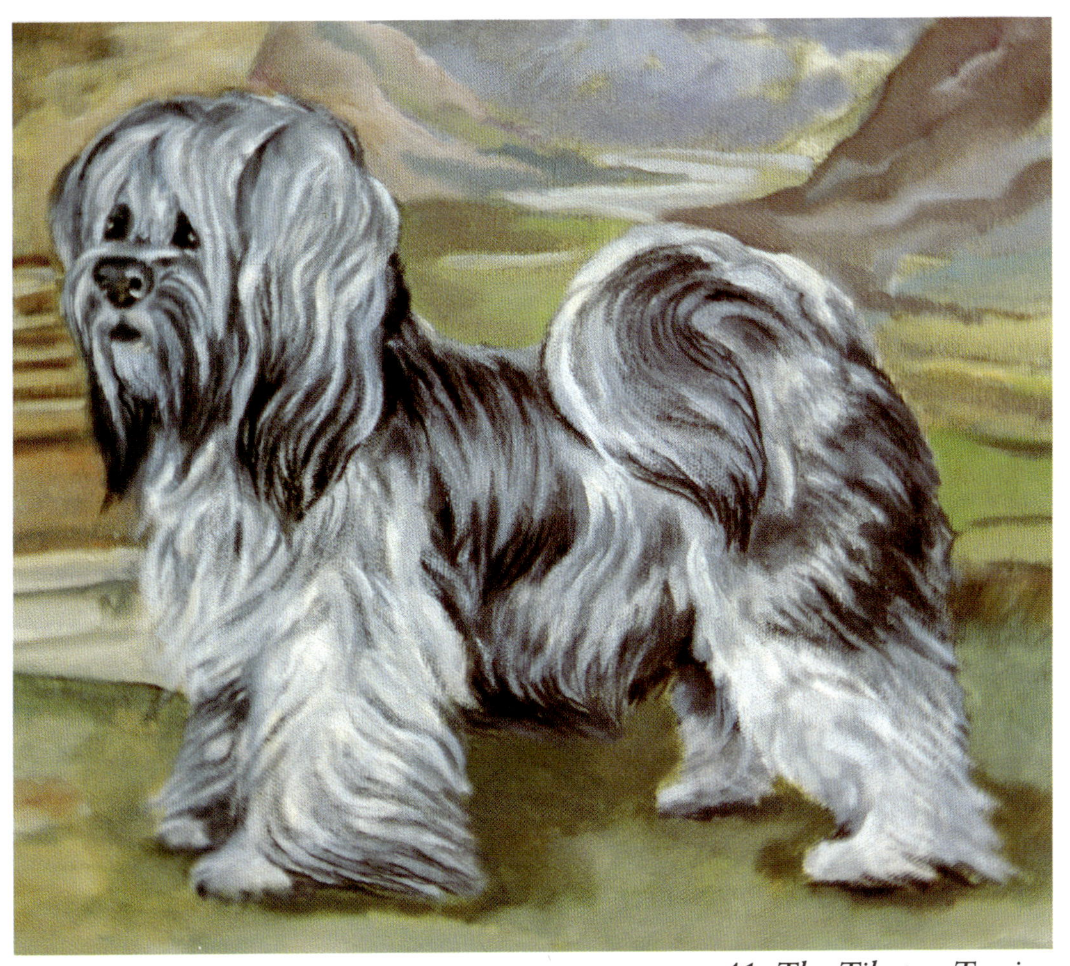

41. *The Tibetan Terrier.*

The Lhasa Apso, one of the original forebears of the Shih Tzu, is also a close relative by more recent association. Some of the first Shih Tzu to be brought to the United States were registered as Lhasa Apsos, and some Lhasa bloodlines have Shih Tzu far back in their family trees. As the present-day Shih Tzu that appear in show rings become larger and larger, the most immediately noticeable difference between them and their Lhasa cousins is in their faces. Shih Tzu are flat-faced dogs with large eyes. Their Lhasa cousins are distinguished principally by longer noses and smaller eyes. Both Shih Tzu and Lhasas come in every possible canine color or colors.

The Tibetan Terrier actually has no terrier blood. He may be fourteen to sixteen inches tall at the shoulder and weigh up to thirty pounds. He is a Lhasa with long legs. Like the Shih Tzu and the Lhasa, he has a heavy coat and may be any color or combination of colors.

The Tibetan Spaniel has been described as "a Pekingese gone wrong." Like the Japanese Chin, he resembles a Pekingese with long legs. Unlike the Pekingese, the Shih Tzu, and the Japanese Chin, however, he is not a flat-faced dog. His muzzle is rather similar to that of an ancestor of the English Toy Spaniel, who three hundred years ago was taken to England via Spain from Japan or China. The Tibetan Spaniel has a double coat which is

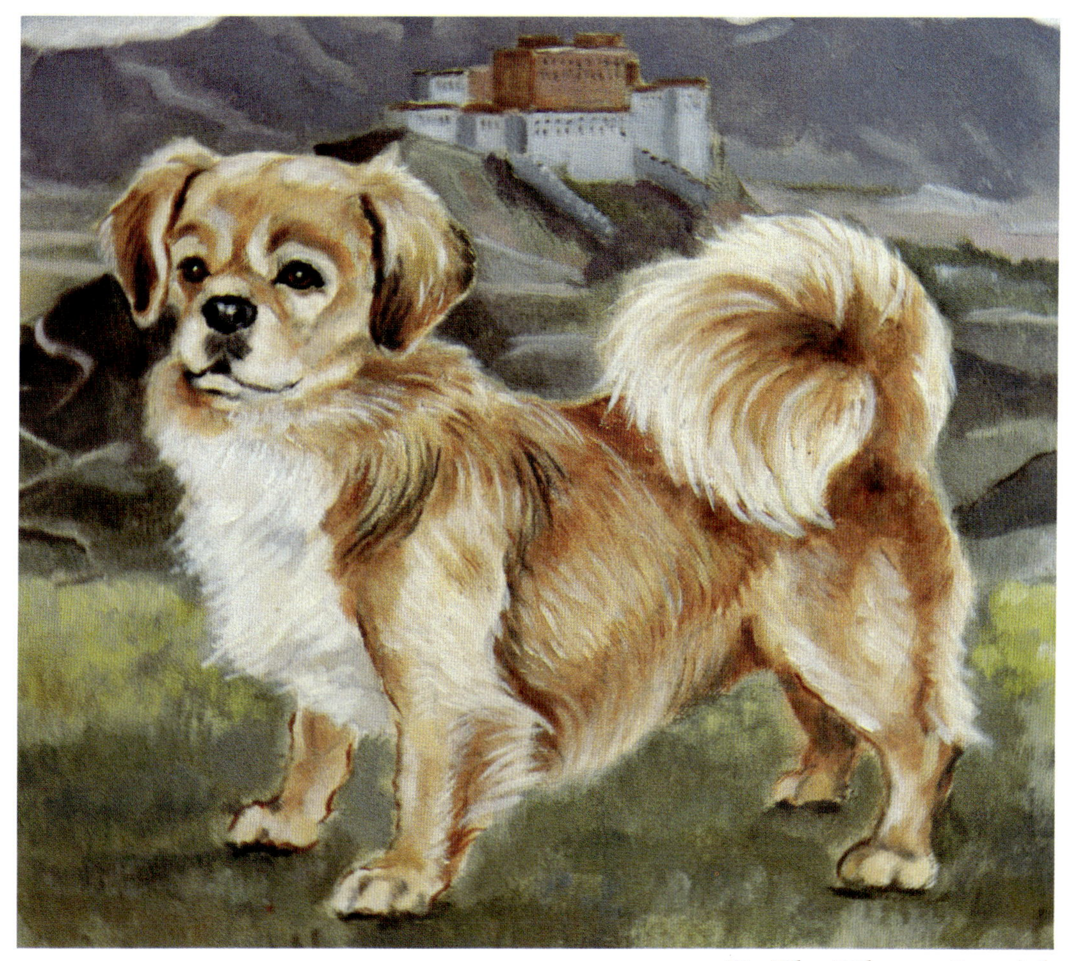

42. The Tibetan Spaniel.

flat and silken in texture and of moderate length. Both the face and the front of the dog's legs are smooth. Dogs of this breed were prized by the Tibetans as alert and spirited watchdogs.

Very close to the hearts of older Tibetans is their legendary snow-lion, the *kang seng*. Known in Tibet even in pre-Buddhist times, the kang seng became the guardian and symbol of Buddhism when he was fused with the Buddha's Indian lion protector. Since the nineteenth century the snow-lion has been the national animal of Tibet. Two kang seng ornament the Tibetan flag, symbolizing the spiritual and temporal functions of the Dalai Lama. This pair of snow-lions is also found on the Dalai Lama's personal seal.

The snow-lion of Tibet is a creature of splendid exuberance, while his mate's milk, legend informs us, is so special that it can only be collected in a golden pot. According to Lama Khenpo Palden Sherab, the snow-lion, whose counterpart on earth is the lion-dog, is white when painted, drawn, or otherwise depicted by traditional Tibetan artists. His mane, tail, claws, and feathering on the backs of the legs are supposed to be turquoise. However, expatriate artists in India and Nepal are inclined to substitute blue or green when weaving him into rugs. Possibly these dye colors are more accessible. Lama Khenpo Palden Sherab says that a golden lion is the mundane denizen of the

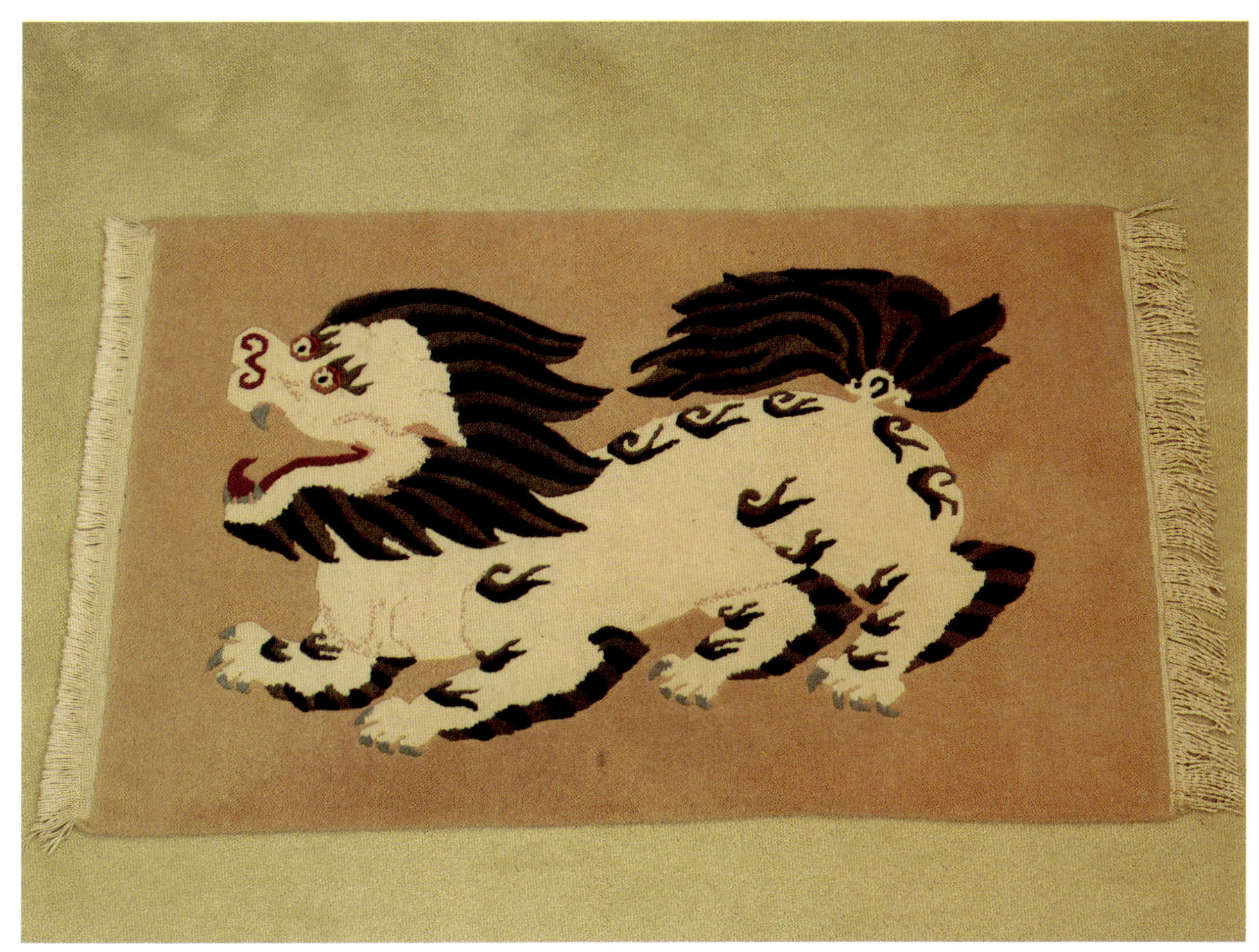

43. A Tibetan rug depicting a kang seng.

earth, an ordinary lion. The Tibetans call him a "muddy lion," or an "on the ground lion."

There is a Tibetan saying, "If the snow-lion stays in the mountains, it is a snow-lion; if it comes down to the plains, it becomes a dog." In his realm among the clouds, the snow-lion has the duty of catching and subduing the dragon. According to Tibetan mythology, the dragon is the creator of thunder, and it is the powerful snow-lion who must keep him in check. In the vicinity of Tsari Ta, the sacred mountain in southern Tibet, near Kang Po, there is no thunder. An ever-vigilant kang seng keeps the dragon firmly controlled, so there is no thunder to disturb the peace of the sacred mountain.

The kang seng distinguishes himself by his ability to adjust his size according to the exigencies of the moment. He may appear as the great steed of the bodhisattva Manjusri, whom the Tibetans call "the gentle-voiced lord." Or he may be the long-haired pet carried under the arm of deity or human.

Spiritual wisdom is the central consideration of Buddhism, and the bodhisattva Manjusri is the guardian of that wisdom. Mounted on his dog-lion, he is greatly venerated and is a favorite subject of Tibetan paintings and bronzes. He is the inspiration of the legions of lamas, or religious teachers, who are the most respected members of the Tibetan population. The snow-lion not only is the steed of Manjusri but also carries the god of good fortune or wealth upon his back.

Tibetan life and art, at least in their traditional forms, can only be truly appreciated in the context of Tibet's unique religion. Every aspect of life was caught up in this elaborate medieval fusion of Buddhism, indigenous mythology, and shamanism. The monastic establishment was the foundation of the government, whose titular head was the Dalai Lama. The Dalai Lama, believed to embody the spirit of the Heart of Wisdom Sutra of Indian Buddhism, is revered as an incarnation of Chenresik (Avalokitesvara). This bodhisattva, beloved in all countries where the Mahayana, or "Great Vehicle," prevails, is to Buddhists what the Madonna is to Catholic Christians.

Buddhism is a tolerant religion, and its teachers have always sought to gather in all beings, all spirits, and all deities. In Tibet every practice leading to the propitiation or the emulation of spirits and deities seems to have found a niche in the Great Vehicle of salvation. Buddhist saints and teachers do not usually attempt to slay demons and devils. Rather, they seek to absorb them and put their energies to work protecting the Buddhist Dharma. The Tibetan pantheon and scriptures are among the most extensive and complicated in the world. Every aspect of traditional Tibetan culture is infused with them.

Tibet is essentially the country of the teacher, or lama. Every serious Tibetan Buddhist who wishes to participate in his religion's most important rites and meditations finds a teacher. Tibetan custom advises that a disciple follow this teacher with unquestioning loyalty, even as a dog follows his master. In both secular and monastic settings, the clan spirit is strong and binds the individual to teacher and religious community for a lifetime. Or possibly, as Tibetan belief maintains, for a series of lifetimes.

Tibetan art is religious art. The Tibetan artist, no matter what his medium, is preoccupied with the ultimate religious experience. Artists serve their deities and the Dharma. Usually they do not sign their creations. A painting or sculpture is dedicated to the spiritual welfare of all beings and to their aspiration to realize their essential buddha-nature. The artist, his lama, and their secular patron unite in the production of a creation which is an act of merit, a vision of religious significance.

In Tibet there is a long tradition of resident painters and sculptors from neighboring countries. Indian, Nepalese, Kashmiri, and Chinese influences appear in sculpture and painting. Iconographic strictures are rigid; painters and sculptors are bound by their demands. Depictions of deities, both benevolent and wrathful, must always conform to intricate traditional standards. In spite of the repetitiousness of subject matter and form, however, Tibetan art is characterized by an ebullient, sometimes even frenzied, energy. The Tibetans love bright colors, particularly red, coral, green, blue, and turquoise, and each of these colors has a spiritual significance. The artist exerts himself to produce a great profusion of detail in his designs. Elaborate decoration and encrustations of brightly colored stones on metal surfaces are found even on articles that are intended for everyday use.

Snow-lions are seen in all forms of Tibetan artistic endeavor. They appear in *thanka* paintings and as bronze figures, as well as on the colorful woolen rugs that even today are still being woven in Tibetan refugee communities in India and Nepal.

The thanka is a painting on cloth, usually cotton or linen rather than the silk preferred by Chinese artists. Thanka means "something rolled up" and may be a banner hung in a Buddhist temple or private chapel or a smaller scroll. These paintings, when the subject is a buddha or an indigenous divinity, may be rolled up to accompany the traveler as he faces the dangers and rigors of his mountainous country. As with scrolls or books of Buddhist scriptures, the divinity in question is believed to impart protection, much as a Saint Christopher medal is expected to aid the Christian voyager.

The kang seng, as depicted in thanka paintings, is a beast of great strength and exuberance. He has enormous paws, thick eyebrows, and a curious spiky ruff framing his face. In one well-known thanka, a pair of dog-lions watch as a man strides off with their tiny cub in his arms. One of these lions is blue, the other cream-colored with a dark coral ruff. "The fair Mount Chimbu is like a lion, blue as turquoise raised in offering to the sky. . . . The Red Crag is like a lion of coral, soaring into the sky."

Tibetan workers in bronze have often been inspired to create the snow-lion in their chosen medium. The sculptures, except when created in China for lamaist temples, are different from those of the Chinese dog-lion. Some bronze snow-lions are elongated and quite exceptionally grotesque. However, an eighteenth-century bronze coin pictured in Giuseppe Tucci's *Tibet: Land of Snows* shows a figure true to the dog-lion type. A compact creature, he is a flat-faced dog-lion, and his expression is one of cheerful benevolence.

Perhaps the most endearing of the snow-lions to be found in Tibetan art are woven into woolen rugs. Carpets and rugs have been made on the steppes of Asia since the dawn of history. Archaeological discoveries in areas covering modern Inner and Outer Mongolia and Tibet predate finds in the Middle East. Knotted pile rugs were preceded by the production of felt. Felt

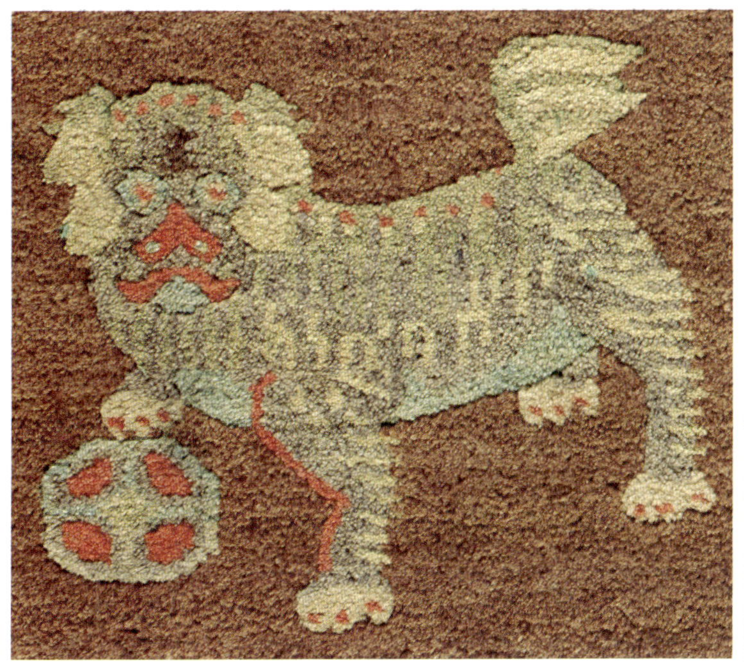

44. *A detail of the dog-lion in plate 45.*

45. *A Tibetan rug with a Chinese-inspired dog-lion in the center.*

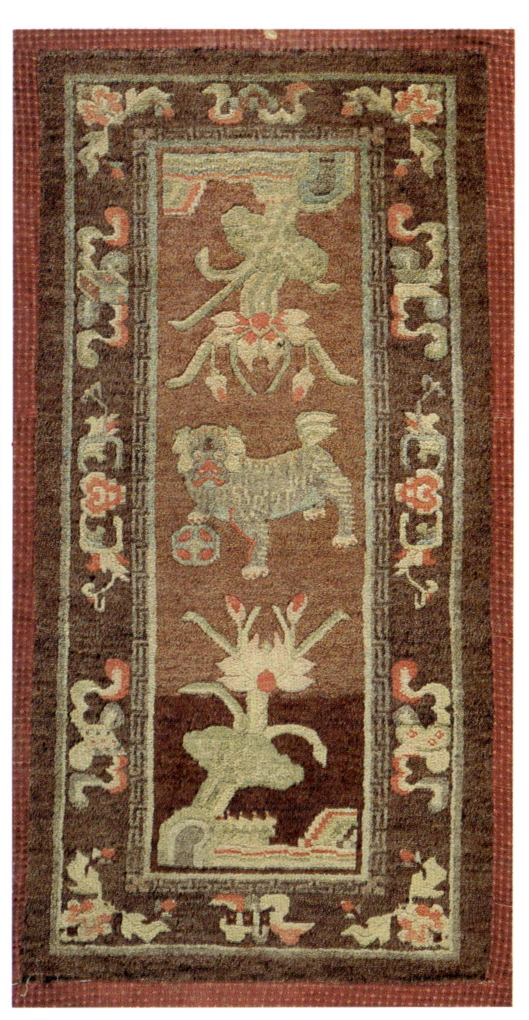

was probably first made by herdsmen, who thereby were able to create cloth and other coverings, including rugs, by compressing the shorn hair of their animals. This cloth was lighter and more flexible than pelts as insulation against the elements. In various qualities and colors, felt was used by Asian nomads to make clothes, boots, blankets, rugs, and tents.

It is uncertain when the techniques of weaving were first used; however, probably it was at least two thousand years ago. The Chinese introduced woven textiles as well as the techniques of spinning and weaving to the nomads of Central Asia. The Tibetans put their carpets to both practical and decorative uses. In Buddhist monasteries piled carpets were used so extensively that one famous lamasery was described by a foreign visitor as "a house of carpets." Carpets, sometimes in layers, covered floors, benches, and walls and were wrapped around pillars. Important lamas were also provided with carpeted seat covers and backrests. Gold, orange, and maroon were highly favored for all sorts of temple furnishings, including carpets.

In everyday life, rich and poor people alike used rugs in dwellings and tents, and even out of doors. Affluent families covered wool-filled cushions with carpets for sleeping or sitting. Divans also were draped with colorful rugs. In winter, floors were blanketed with many layers of felt and wool, on top of which carpets were laid as decoration. In summer, called in Tibetan "the time of gardens," rugs and cushions were placed in courtyards and in tents and under awnings. Here people gathered to watch the performance of plays and dances.

Essential to Tibetan life were horses and mules, and they were not neglected by native weavers. Ornamental additions to harness, such as neck bands and covers for bridles and cruppers, were common, as were the mats that underlay and covered saddles. Mounts of rich personages and important lamas were covered with pile horse blankets while resting or while, riderless, following a moving caravan. Snow-lions decorate at least three interesting under-saddle rugs displayed in an exhibition at the Textile Museum, in Washington, D.C. One curious example is a snow-lioness with an atypical worried expression and stylized breasts. Apparently she fed her offspring in a more conventional manner than the Chinese dog of Fo, whose babies were thought to drink milk from their mother's long claws.

Tibetan mats, rugs, and carpets are made from wool fleece with an occasional admixture of yak or goat hair. In China, one way to wash the fleece was to soak it in goat's urine. In another method, a basket was lined with leaves and filled with ashes, through which water was percolated. The resulting potion was tested with a hen's egg. The egg was used as a primitive hydrometer, and was obliged to float at a certain level when the concoction was ready for use. After being laundered, the wool was rinsed and dried in the sun. The Tibetans did not do such a thorough cleaning of their wool, which was simply rinsed in cold water to which dried fruit might be added.

Traditionally, the Tibetans obtained their dyes from Indian or Chinese indigo, madder from Bhutan and Nepal, and Tibetan walnuts, wild saffron, barberry, gooseberries, and rhubarb roots. Madder and saffron produced reds, barberry and rhubarb were used for yellow dyes, and walnuts were used to produce shades of brown. Some synthetic dyes have been used since the late nineteenth century. Until very recently, all refugee rugs were made from machine-spun Indian yarn. Only within the last fifteen years or so has there been a revival of homespun yarns colored with vegetable dyes.

Tibetans use many Chinese designs in their rugs: dragons, phoenixes, clouds, medallions, and flowers. Religious symbols, such as the Buddhist cosmic-cross design, the lotus, and the *vajra,* or diamond, are particularly favored. Dragons coil around the great pillars of temple halls. One lamaist temple in China's Qinghai Province, a structure of wood and earth, required 168 pillars to support its enormous roof. These pillars were wrapped with rugs of vivid dragon designs on a yellow ground.

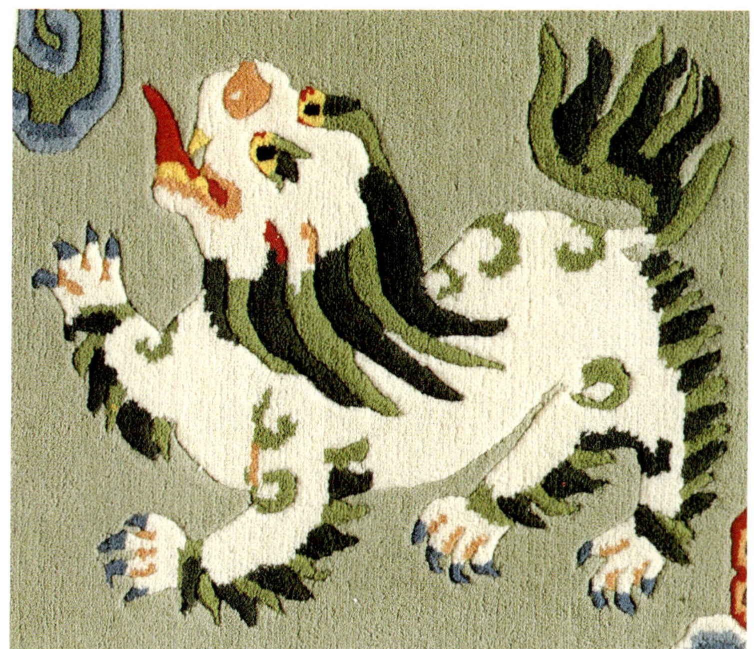

46. *A detail of the snow-lion in plate 47.*

47. *A Tibetan rug depicting the face of a mythical makara surrounded by a snow-lion, tiger, dragon, and eagle.*

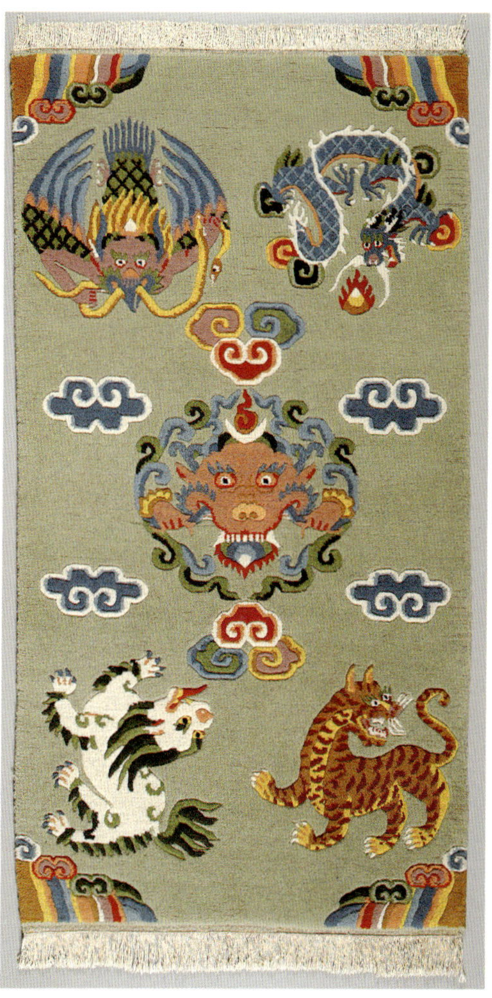

The dog-lion is far more frequently used in Tibetan than in Chinese carpet design. He may prance alone on a small square prayer mat, or he may be accompanied by other creatures, real and mythic, amid fanciful curly clouds or waves on a larger carpet. The Chinese dog of Fo is usually dignified and sedate, as befits his role of protector. The Japanese shishi is a playful and humorous fellow. The Tibetan creature is spirit unfettered, of electric energy. He is often in motion, appearing about to scale the highest Himalayan peak or even to ascend to the firmament itself.

The fusion of dog and snow-lion in Tibet did not bring the celestial creature permanently down to earth. He remains free to navigate the heavens with dazzling strength and speed. However, he also has the capacity to reveal himself as the small, cheerful companion of bed and hearth.

DOGS, OTHER NON-HUMAN BEINGS, AND BUDDHISM

Since the lion-dog has long been known as the dog of Buddha, the Fu or Fo dog, it is appropriate for the reader to learn more about the place of four-legged beings in the Buddhist tradition. But first a slight digression is in order as we observe the place of non-human beings in some philosophies of East and West other than Buddhism which have affected the lives and fate of all four-legged creatures down through the centuries. Art and myth do not arise in a vacuum but are integral parts of the cultural ethos which creates them.

Unlike most peoples of the ancient world, the Egyptians

loved animals and shared their homes, temples, tombs, and salvation with them. The dog-headed god Anubis welcomed the righteous to the underworld, according to the Book of the Dead. Cats, dogs, and other animals accompanied the dead to their new life, where it was expected that all would exist together in peace and harmony. The Hebrews despised all things Egyptian, including their kindred feelings for animals. This prejudice is reflected in the Jewish and Christian scriptures and probably was responsible for some medieval European attitudes toward non-human beings. In fact, much of this prejudice still survives in most of the modern world.

The Persian adherents of the Parsi religion, which prevailed in Persia from pre-Christian times till Persia's conquest by the second successor of Mohammed, loved and venerated dogs. One of the sacred books in the Zend Avesta is given over to the subject of the dog. Here is a quotation from this scripture: "I, Ahura Mazda have made the dog strong of body against the evil-doer, and watchful over your goods, when he is of sound mind. If these two dogs of mine, the shepherd's dog and the house dog, pass by the house of any of my faithful people, let them never be kept away from it. For no house could subsist on earth made by Ahura, but for those two dogs of mine, the shepherd's dog and the house dog."

The writer of the scripture describes the proper care and treatment of dogs in careful detail: "If the bones stick in the dog's teeth or stop in his throat, or if the hot food burn his mouth or his tongue, so that mischief follows therefrom, and the dog dies, this is a sin."

Now we must turn to the Hebraic and Hellenic cultures, which influenced the morality of both the modern West and the westernized East, in order to understand the place of the non-human in theology and contemporary thought. The ancient Hebrews were not without respect for nature and for particular beasts, such as the useful sheep and ox. For canines, however, the Hebrews had nothing but contempt. Dogs, according to the Book of Revelation, would be excluded from the New Jerusalem. This attitude seems also to characterize Moslem sentiments toward canine beings. The Hebrew worldview placed man at the center of the universe. Man was believed to be the creation of a patriarchal deity who supplied his restless progeny with the rest of creation to use according to their whim.

Hellenic infusions into the New Testament further emphasized man as the apex of creation. Man is the temple of the Holy Spirit, a singular piece of work slated for the eternal life of salvation. The idea of Christian stewardship of other living beings in theory involves proper use and care of "resources," as all other living things are labeled by some modern Christians. In practice, this ideal has not provided either living things or their environment with adequate protection from the greed of and destruction by humanity.

Perusal of the myths of the ancient Greeks persuades the student of history that considerable ambivalence toward the animal world was a predominant theme. In the chapters in which the mythological animals of China and Japan are described, it is pointed out that many of these creatures are symbols of desirable qualities or, as with the baku, are thought to be man's helpers. They may be even paragons of religious virtue, like the gentle qilin/kirin.

Composite creatures existed in the mythology of Greece, as in that of China and Japan. An exceptional creature, portrayed as benevolent, was the instructor of Jason. This centaur was a wise teacher. Special too was Pegasus, the winged horse, who was favored by the Greek gods and was the bearer of lightning and thunder.

On the other hand, the Greek writer Hesiod wrote of demonic monsters that thrived on blood and mayhem. The part-animal deities described in his *Theogony* are nightmarish visions, sometimes consisting of portions of various beasts in combination with parts of human anatomy. Along with snakes,

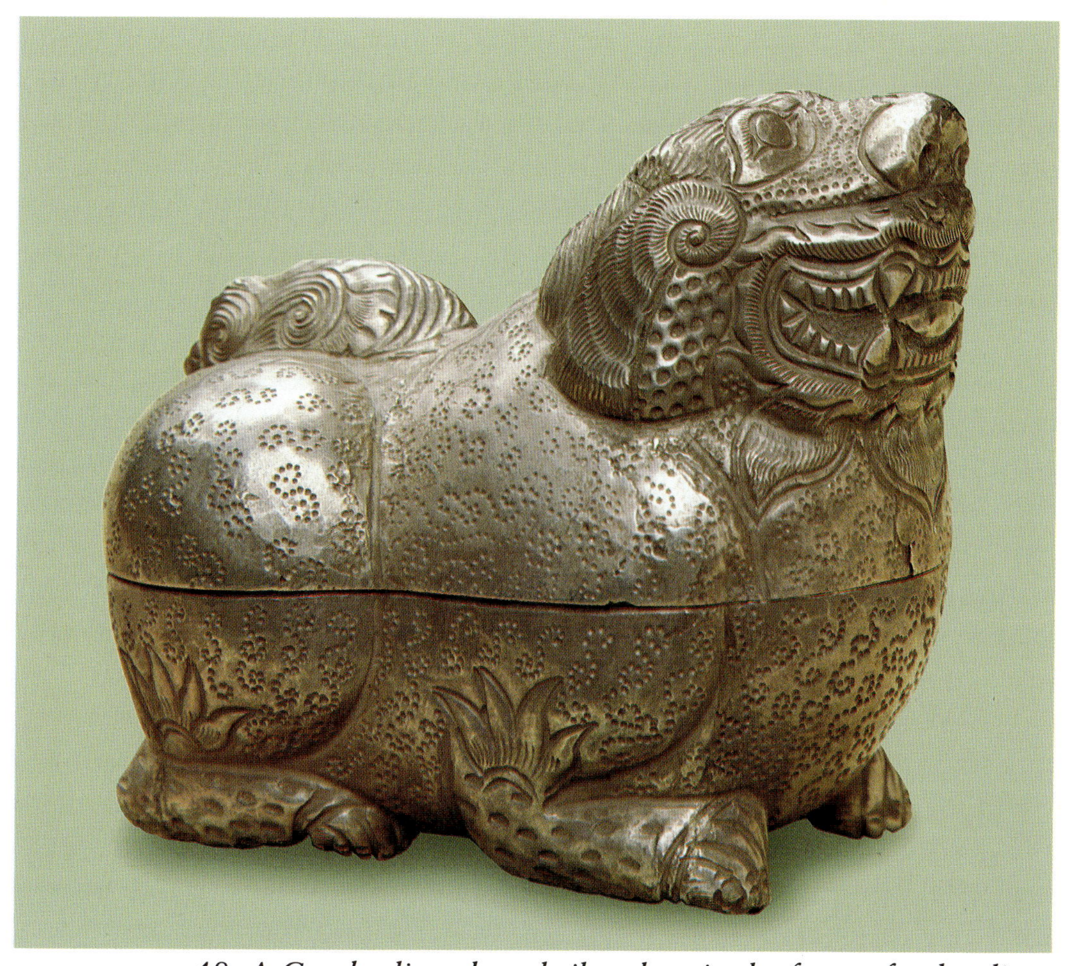

48. *A Cambodian chased silver box in the form of a dog-lion.*

dragons, and other creatures real or imaginary, whose origins were often outside Greece, this legion of grotesque creations inspired hatred and fear. Many of the composite animals appeared centuries later in European legends and fairy tales, where, in combination with primitive Biblical views, they were responsible for much of the European fear and contempt of intimacy with the animal world.

It has been suggested that the distaste aroused by speculations on strange monsters was caused by the belief that animal-human couplings, not infrequent in early European farm communities, might be responsible for the appearance of blood-thirsty animal-humans. Apprehension about the birth of deformed offspring evolved into fear of monsters and mistrust of animals in general. The Christian devil, perhaps inspired by the god Pan, was believed to be a creature with a goat's legs and hooves.

Now for a few reflections on the place of the canine creature in England, which since the eighteenth century has been a center for a humane ethic for the Western world. Christian philosophies cannot be said to have played an important part in the feelings that the English have for four-legged creatures, particularly for their dogs. The Welsh historian Keith Thomas has described in absorbing detail the development, between 1500 and 1800, of a deeper sensibility and of the recognition of the kinship of all creatures. During this period some theologians relinquished rigid dogmas of man's functions and place in nature, and naturalists and scientists began to question the existence of boundaries between man and other animals.

Not only four-legged animals were considered inferior beings. The question of whether the human female possessed a soul was more or less seriously debated in English theological circles in the sixteenth century. The animal aspects of childbearing rendered her humanity questionable. Even infants seemed more animal than human, according to one Jacobean writer quoted by Thomas: "What is an infant but a brute beast in the shape of a man?"

By the seventeenth century, English moralists were debating man's right to slaughter four-legged beings for food. The philosophy of the ancient Greek thinker Pythagoras was widely disseminated in English intellectual circles through translations of Ovid's *Metamorphoses*. Pythagoras is believed to have been acquainted with translations of the spiritual philosophies of Hinduism.

Western man has always relied heavily on a diet of his fellow creatures. Until recent medical discoveries of ailments induced or stimulated by overindulgence in meat eating, the intake of flesh by northern Europeans and North Americans was enormous. In *Scenes of Childhood* Sylvia Townsend Warner gives a traditional English recipe for "cottage stew." The ingredients: three or four partridges, a hare, a fowl, a pheasant, two pounds of beefsteak, and thick slices of green bacon, all seasoned with vegetables, herbs, and a teapotful of port.

An enormous market not only for meat but also for pelts and hides has existed since the earliest times. This has been an integral part of European history, particularly in the countries of northern Europe. Uses both essential and frivolous have caused vast populations of animals, both wild and domestic, to perish. One might recall that in the fifteenth century, production of thirty copies of the Gutenberg Bible, printed on vellum (calfskin) and bound with calf hides, required the demise of five thousand calves.

As members of a favored few among four-legged beings, the little lion-dogs' European relations were allowed to participate in this conspicuous consumption as they shared the gastronomic fortunes of ladies of means and leisure. The Pekingese, who in the fifteenth century may have resembled the present-day Japanese Chin, probably graced the splendid chambers of the ladies of Venice. The Toy Spaniel, a distant cousin of the Pekingese, was a favorite at all European courts. In the seventeenth century

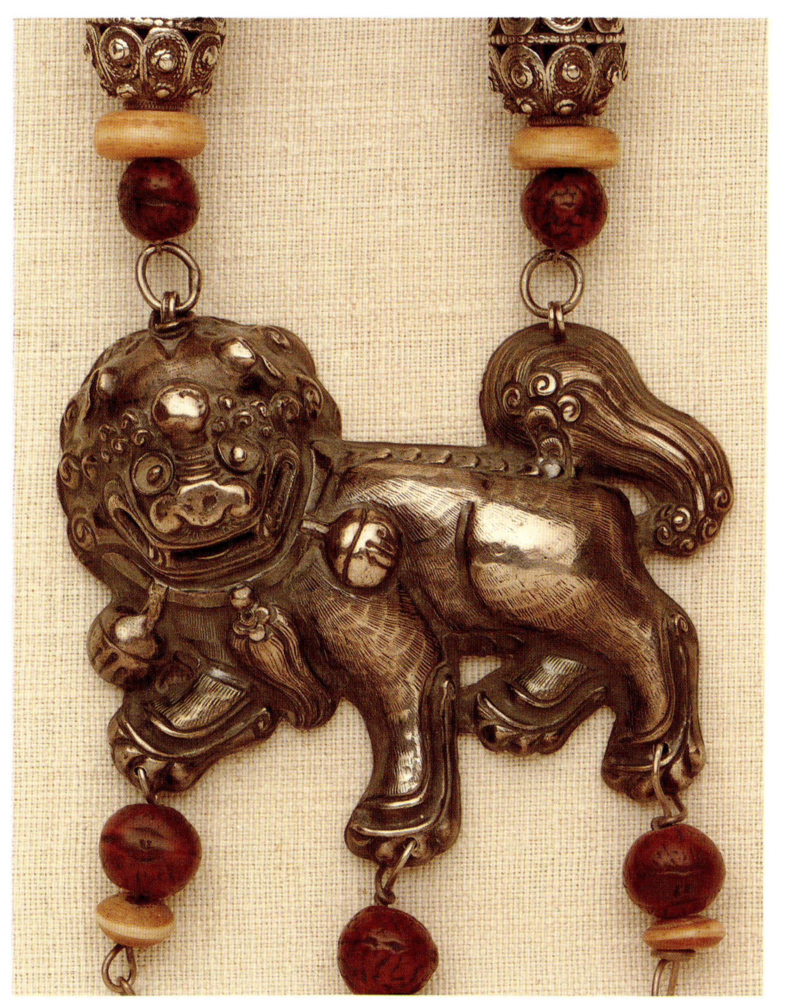

49. *A silver incense holder from China in the form of a dog-lion.*

the Pug, also related to the Pekingese, became the favored companion of European ladies. According to Thomas, preachers in England occasionally complained that children were neglected by their mothers, who preferred the company of small four-legged companions. The same writer also maintains that by the mid-nineteenth century "there was no civilized land 'where the canine race is more the companion of man than in Great Britain or any nation which has so many varieties of it.'"

Western science inherited from the Semitic religions and from Greek philosophy a homocentric approach to living beings as well as to their use in research. And just as medieval clerics were prone to torment fellow humans to save their souls, scientists, particularly in the field of medicine, are still inclined to believe that two-legged bodies should be saved by the sacrifice of four-legged bodies.

In the seventeenth century the French philosopher René Descartes asserted that an animal is a machine, an automaton. Like a clock, it has no consciousness; it is incapable of thought or emotion and, appearances to the contrary, experiences neither pleasure nor pain. Cartesian scientists vivisected fully conscious dogs and maintained that their cries were only the noise of a little spring that had been activated and that the dogs' bodies were without feeling. Modern successors to this mind-set savage and butcher sixty million non-humans a year in laboratories in the United States.

In the three great religions of India, Hinduism, Buddhism, and Jainism, there is a teaching called *ahimsa*. This Sanskrit term, which may be roughly translated as "noninjury," expresses a concept with many implications. The practice of ahimsa involves strenuous efforts to avoid doing harm to any living thing and is applied to every form of life. Man is not the center of all things. He shares his divine spark with all beings: "The wise look upon a Brahmana possessed of learning and humility, on a cow, an elephant, a dog, and a svapaka as alike." This "alike" is applied to spiritual value rather than to the mundane characteristics of species, appearance, or behavior.

In India during the reign of the Buddhist emperor Asoka, more than two hundred years before the Christian era, ahimsa involved the planting of banyan trees to provide shade for man and beast, the planting of mango groves for food, and the creation of rest houses and watering places for the comfort of all along well-traveled routes. Ahimsa proscribes the killing or even injuring of any creature. To cause death or injury to any living thing is believed to create bad karma, misfortune, for the perpetrator. "As you sow, so shall you reap" is perhaps one Western way of expressing the idea.

The first precept, or commandment, of Buddhism is abstinence from killing or injury. However, many Asian and some Western Buddhists have devised various justifications for the killing of animals as well as the eating of meat. These justifications, though widely accepted, especially in modern times, are based on human expediency and inclination.

The sayings and commandments of the Buddha, like the sayings of Jesus of Nazareth, do not exist in their original form and were only written down after the death of the Great Teacher. The Buddha spoke Magadhi, an ancient Indian language. The scriptures of Southern and Northern Buddhism are written in Pali and Sanskrit, respectively. Though there are divergences in the interpretations of the precepts and in the accounts of episodes in the life of the Enlightened One, the spirit of the tradition is plain. The texts, whether Pali or Sanskrit or their translations into Burmese, Thai, Chinese, Tibetan, and Japanese, all attest to the Buddha's respect for all beings and his desire for their protection.

One scripture of Northern, or Mahayana, Buddhism, is the Lankavatara Sutra. A chapter of this sutra is devoted to condemnation of meat eating. Here are a few excerpts: "Thus Mahamati, wherever there is the evolution of living beings let people cherish the thought of kinship with them, and, thinking that all beings are [to be loved as if they were] an only child, let

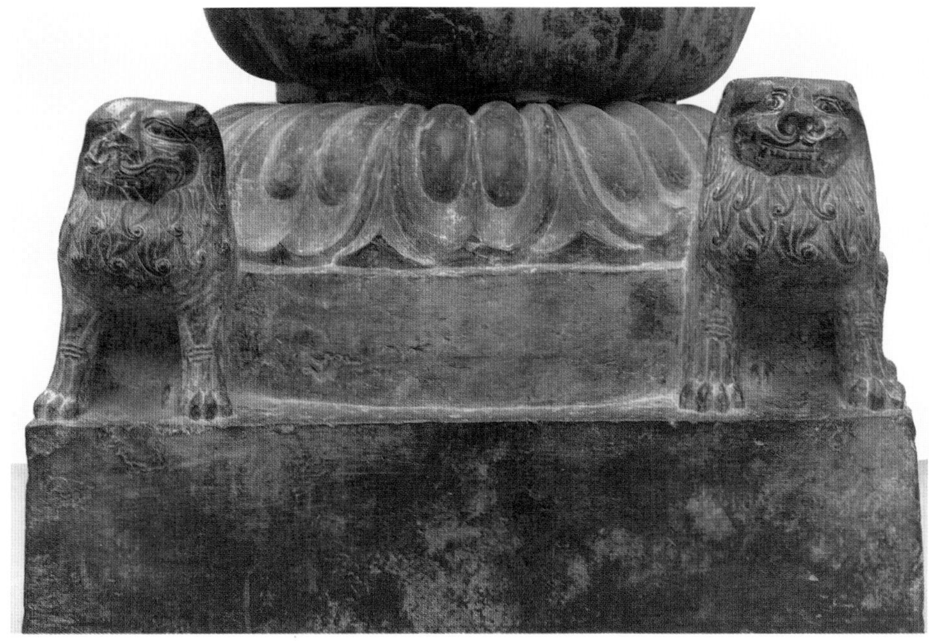

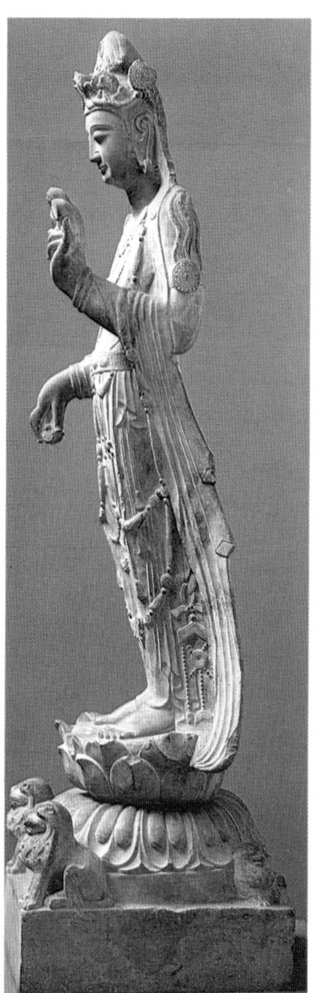

50. *A detail of two dog-lions in plate 51. Courtesy, Museum of Fine Arts, Boston; Asiatic Curators Fund.*

51. *A Chinese polychrome stone statue of Guanyin, bodhisattva of compassion, guarded by dog-lions; ca.* A.D. *580. Courtesy, Museum of Fine Arts, Boston; Asiatic Curators Fund.*

them refrain from eating meat." And further: "Mahamati, there is generally an offensive odor to a corpse, which goes against nature; therefore, let the Bodhisattva refrain from eating meat. Mahamati, when flesh is burned, whether it be that of a dead man or of some other creature, there is no distinction in the odour. When flesh of either kind is burned, the odour emitted is equally noxious. . . . There may be some . . . people in the future . . . who being under the influence of the . . . taste for meat, they will string together in various ways some sophistic arguments to defend meat-eating. . . . Meat-eating . . . I do not permit." That which one does not wish inflicted upon oneself should not be inflicted upon others.

Now let us turn to Buddhist history and a few examples of concern for four-legged beings inspired by the ethic of Buddhism and by ahimsa.

The Buddhist emperor Asoka, who ruled India from 265 to 238 B.C., is perhaps the only ruler in recorded history who not only decreed compassion for all, humans and animals, but also left a record of his interpretation of Buddhist morality engraved in stone for future generations to observe. From the Rock and Pillar edicts, as they are known, we learn that Asoka fought a particularly bloody war in which he conquered Kalinga, a country on the coast of the Bay of Bengal. Thereafter he renounced war and devoted his imperial energies to the propagation of the Dharma. For him, Buddhist teaching and practice were synonymous with Buddhist morality. Each person had to work out his own salvation and "eat the fruit of his deeds." The heart of the Dharma as proclaimed in the edicts was an amalgam of duty, compassion, tolerance, and truthfulness. Asoka dispatched missionaries all over India and Sri Lanka, as well as to the realms of Epirus, Syria, Macedonia, Cyrene, and Egypt. These missionaries were also expected to impart medical advice on remedies for man and beast.

The first of the celebrated Rock Edicts of Asoka, which has been found in six locations in India, reads in part: "Here [in the capital] no animal may be slaughtered for sacrifice. . . . Formerly, in the kitchen of His . . . Majesty the King, from day to day many hundred thousands of living creatures were slaughtered for savoury meats. But now when this Edict is being written, there are slaughtered [daily] . . . only three living creatures, to wit, two peacocks and one antelope . . . the antelope, however, not invariably. Even these three living creatures in future shall not be slaughtered."

A later edict involves restrictions on the mutilation, that is, branding and castrating, of animals and further forbids the burning of forests, since life will thereby be destroyed. Female creatures with young, and their offspring up to six months of age, may not be killed, nor may any animal not needed for food.

The second Rock Edict describes positive steps taken by the emperor to improve the lot of humans and non-humans: "Everywhere has . . . the king made two kinds of curative arrangements, to wit, curative arrangements for men and curative arrangements for beasts. Medicinal herbs [for man and beast], . . . wherever they were lacking, have been imported and planted.

"On the roads both wells have been dug and trees planted for the enjoyment of man and beast."

Thus did Asoka plan for the welfare of beings throughout his realm. Minor Rock Edict II gives us an interesting indication of the relative importance of human duty toward animals in Asokan Buddhism: "Father and mother must be hearkened to; similarly, respect for living creatures must be firmly established; truth must be spoken. These are the virtues of the Law . . . which must be practised."

The above-mentioned edicts are only a few of the many that were carved in caves and on rocks and pillars across Asoka's empire. Massive polished stone pillars marked pilgrims' routes and places associated with events in the life of the Buddha. The most impressive of the Asokan edict pillars is located in Bihar State at Lauriya Nandangarh, not far from the border of Nepal. This polished sandstone column rises thirty-two feet in height, and its weight has been estimated at close to fifty tons. Crowning the pillar is an impressive statue of a lion.

Some scholars believe that such monumental pillars, which are indigenous to India, evolved from a pre-Buddhist cult of a cosmic column, the *axis mundi*. It is possible that these Indian pillars inspired the lion-crowned pillars found in cemeteries, as well as on bridges and in front of stores, in China.

For many centuries after the death of the Enlightened One, Chinese and Korean monks made the difficult pilgrimage to India to study with famous Buddhist teachers and to acquire scriptures to take back to their own countries. The pilgrims recorded in some detail the customs they encountered in the lands through which they traveled.

One such pilgrim was an eighth-century monk from Korea. Huei Chao went to China to study Buddhism before his twentieth year. From China he set out on a pilgrimage which was to take him through India and Central Asia. A fragment of his travel journal was discovered in a cave in Dunhuang, in the far west of Gansu Province, China. Founded in A.D. 366, the Dunhuang cave-temple complex became one of the largest and richest Buddhist settlements in Asia. At the beginning of this century, many hundreds of paintings, embroideries, and Buddhist scriptures in several languages were discovered there in a long-sealed room, along with the journal fragment. This document was presented to the Musée Guimet, in Paris, around 1908 and is now in the Bibliothèque Nationale. The journal provides some information on the state of Buddhism in northeastern India, Afghanistan, and the two Turkestans more than five centuries before Marco Polo and the Chinese texts of the Mongolian Yuan dynasty.

The intrepid monk followed "hanging mountain paths" and was buffeted by snowstorms with icy winds tearing "into the Earth's cracks." Marauding bandits and unfriendly rhinoceroses and tigers were a constant threat. Impressed by the Asokan pillars at Varanasi, he tells us that the lion-topped pillars were "very magnificent; five men together could encircle them."

Huei Chao also tells us that in the five Indian states "there are no wooden neck collars [for criminals], bastinado, or jails. Whoever commits a crime is punished by fines according to the gravity [of the crime]: also there is no death penalty. Up to the king and down to the common man, one sees nothing of beat-hunts or hunts with falcons and hounds. Now, on the roads [there are] of course highway robbers. Still they rob only possessions, leaving [the people] then free, not killing them."

Huei Chao continues: in Central India "the people eat non-

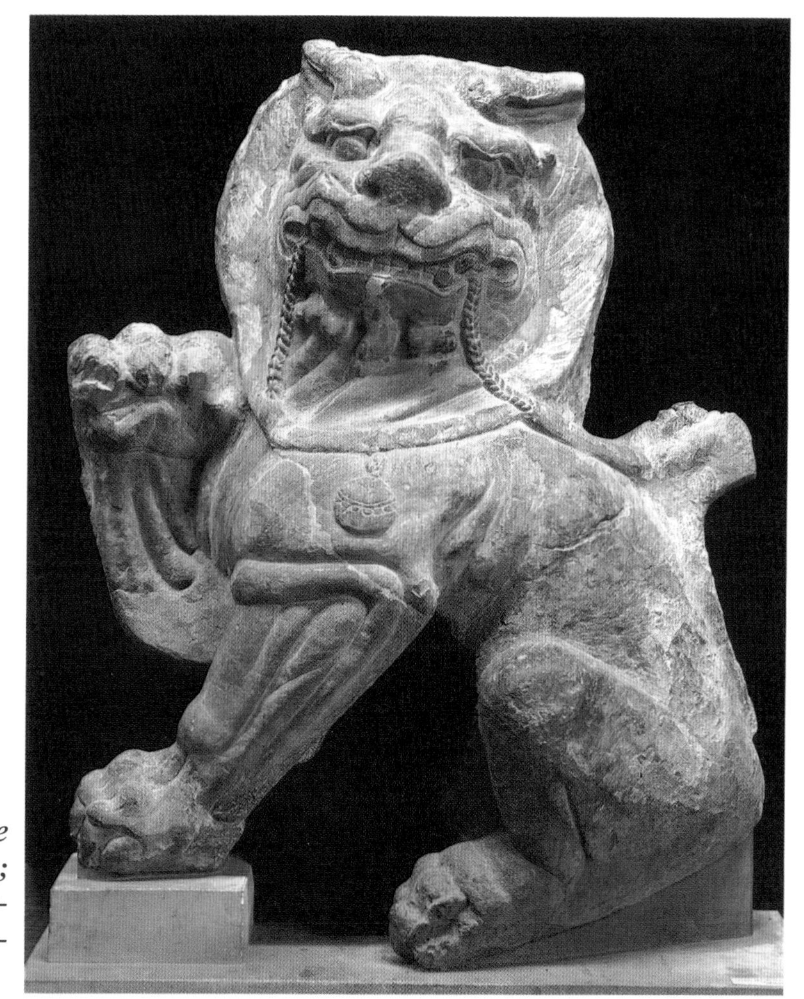

52. *A limestone lion from the cave-temples of Longmen, China; late seventh century* A.D. *Courtesy, Museum of Fine Arts, Boston; Rebecca R. Joslin Fund.*

sticky rice, corn, bread-cakes, steamed doughwares and melted butter, milk, and cream." Furthermore, "the inhabitants are good and do not care much for killing," and "in the stores of the city one sees no places where there are butcher shops and where meat is sold."

North of Gandhara, the monk discovered that though the king piously venerated the Buddhist teaching, and though he, the royal wives, and the princes built cloisters and made many gifts to the Buddhist community, the city unfortunately contained "many people with bad professions. In the stores of the cities there are many butchers."

One rather curious custom was that the king of this region twice annually presented the Buddhist monastic community with camels, elephants, gold, silver, furniture, and women. For the women and the elephants, the king permitted the monks to fix a price, which he then duly paid, whereupon the elephants and the women once again became the king's property. It seems that even in the region of the country of the Enlightened One's birth there arose many different, and sometimes peculiar, ways of living with the Buddhist teachings.

Homocentric non-Buddhists find it surprising that in Buddhist temples services are conducted for other species. Funeral and memorial rituals are considered appropriate and natural. In

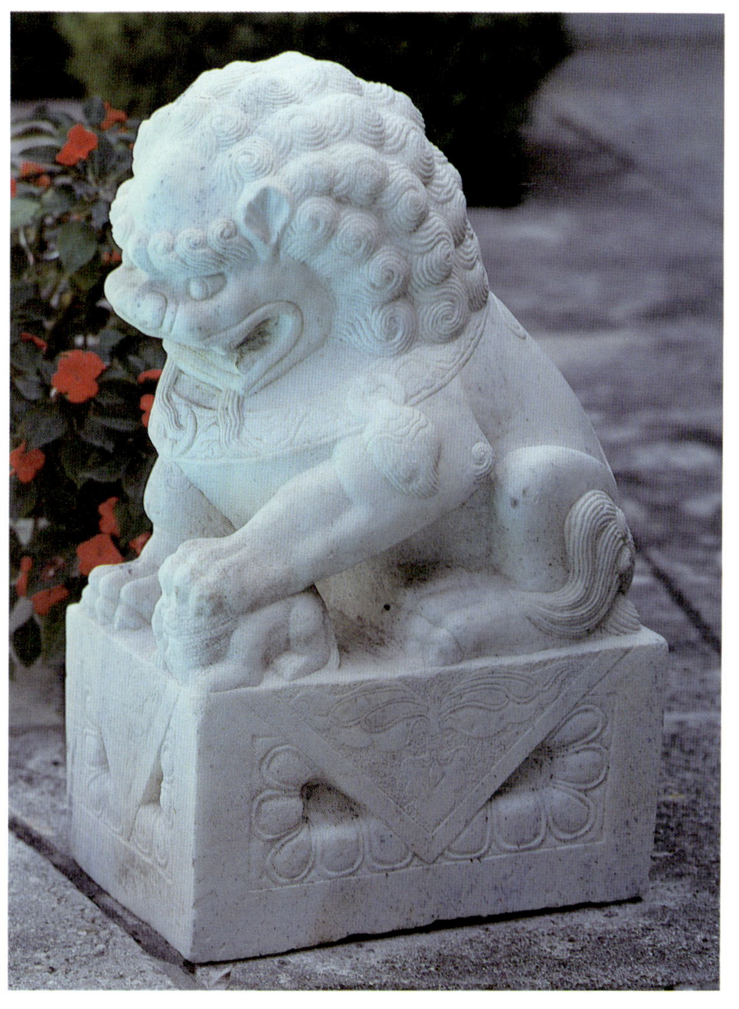

53. *A white stone mother Fu dog and offspring.*

Japan there are rituals for cows, pigs, fish, and animals used in research. As one Japanese Buddhist priest writes: "Out of necessity we kill other beings to survive," but "we should not forget to extend our deep feelings of gratitude to those we kill. . . . Through rituals we try to emphasize and confirm our appreciation of the value of all beings."

An example of such a ritual conducted in a large Buddhist temple in Japan has been reported in the Western press. The ceremony, attended by government officials as well as by executives and employees of one of Japan's largest corporations, was a memorial service for the fifteen thousand whales that had been slaughtered to feed Japanese people during a three-year period. The participants worked for the largest Japanese whaling company, and they joined the monks in the chanting of sutras for the enlightenment of the whales they had killed.

Since present-day Westerners generally have no taste for whale meat and are dedicated to the preservation of the largest and one of the most intelligent of the earth's mammals, this memorial service appears to be a hypocritical exercise, especially since not even popular Japanese Buddhism excuses wasteful and unnecessary killing. The enormous and brutal massacres of Japanese factory whalers obviously are not necessary to Japanese survival. However, like humans everywhere, Japanese Buddhists who consume whale meat have their blind spots, as well as that all-too-human capacity for overlooking cruelty when their appetites are involved.

A Western press report of a funeral in the Buddhist country of Sri Lanka describes an event more comprehensible to the Western mentality. For fifty-one years an elephant had participated in a religious pageant during which he transported a relic of the Buddha on his back. In return for his many years of faithful service, Raja the elephant was accorded an official state funeral.

In both China and Japan there have always been special Buddhist temples dedicated to bodhisattvas or patron deities who are considered protectors of animals. Some of these temples have graveyards where the ashes of companion animals may be buried. At Jikei-in, a temple in a suburb of Tokyo, pets may be cremated and buried in an adjoining cemetery that contains many fine tombs. Sutras are chanted for departed dogs and cats, and an image of Kannon (Avalokitesvara) Bodhisattva, the spirit of compassion, presides over the room where owners bid farewell to their animal friends.

In China at the turn of the century there was a temple devoted to the protector of canines. On the first and fifteenth of the month, Chinese dog owners might pray for the well-being of

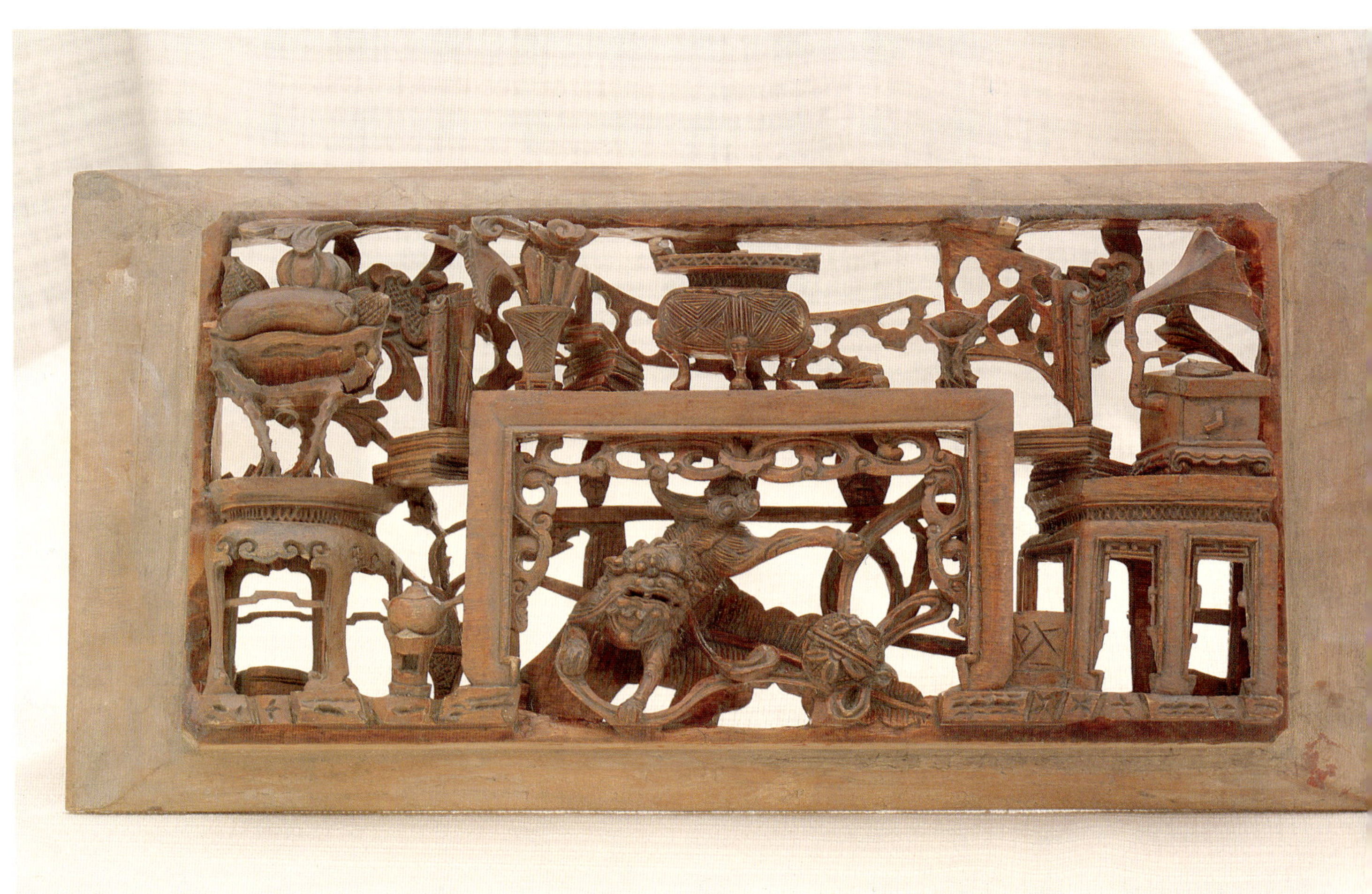

54. A Chinese wood tile depicting an altar, tables, and a Fo dog.

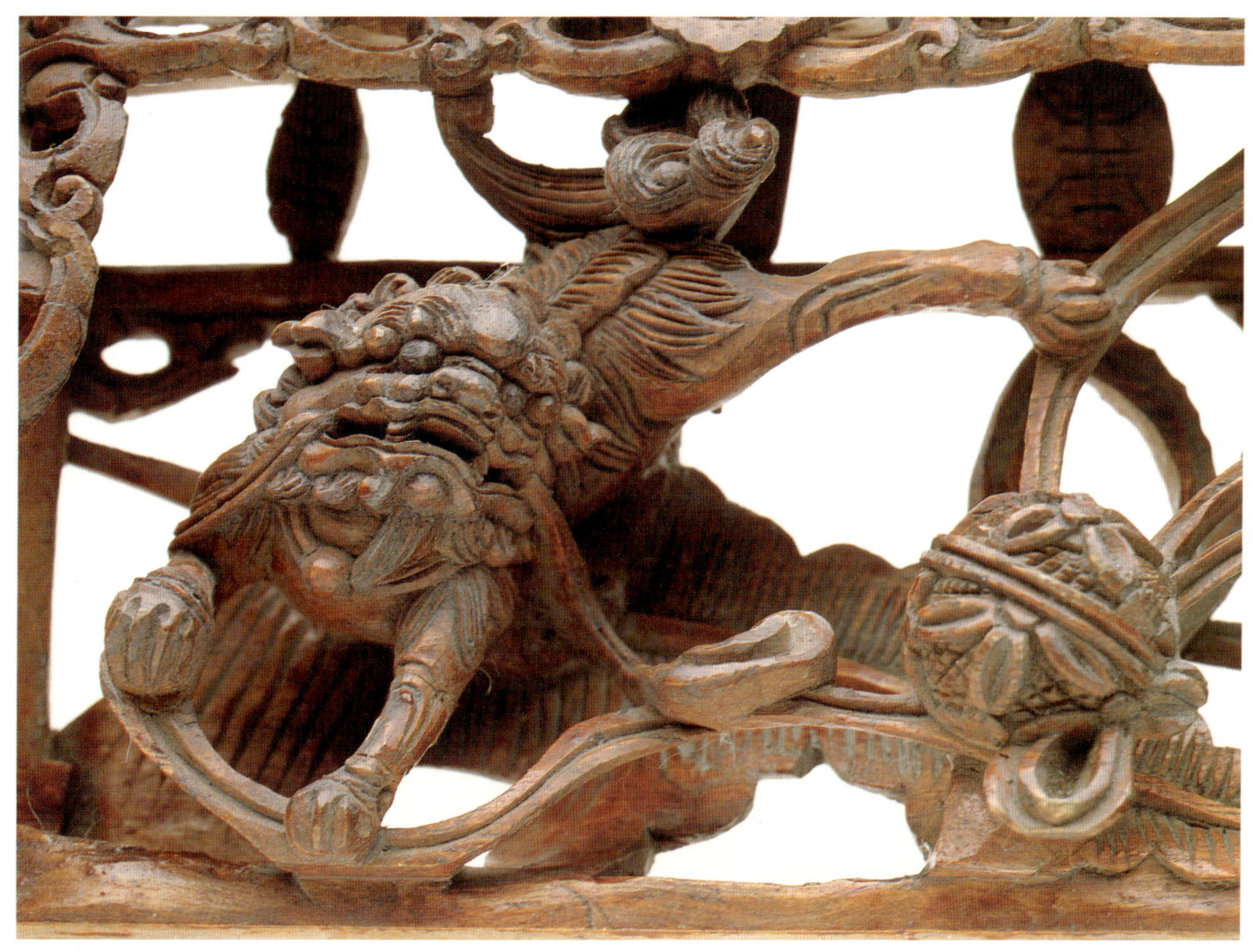

55. A detail of the Fo dog in plate 54.

their four-footed friends. If a dog was in danger of death, the owner placed a small clay image of a dog on the altar. This substitute was believed to persuade the presiding bodhisattva or deity that the ailing dog should be allowed to spend more time on earth in the company of the fond owner. A blessing on the clay form was thought to be transferable to the flesh-and-blood dog.

In the spectacular *nehan,* or nirvana, paintings of Japan, depictions of the Buddha's last hours on earth, humans are not the only mourners. Assembled is every sort of four-legged being, large and small, to mourn the departure of the Great Teacher. In the nehan paintings of the thirteenth century, a large dog-lion is seen. Sometimes he is seated. Or he may assume other poses, such as lying on his back with all four legs waving in the air, as he expresses his distress at the passing of One whose teaching has brought glimmers of hope for peace and good treatment to four-legged beings through many centuries of turbulent human history.

Here the story of the lion-dog must end. However, this discourse is concluded with the hope that the next time the reader sees a dog-lion image while sightseeing in an Asian land, on a museum tour, at the gates of a Western Chinatown, or as a decoration in a friend's home or office, perhaps his or her attention will linger for a few moments and some aspects of the history of the dog-lion/lion-dog will be recalled. Perhaps an encounter with a Shih Tzu, a Pekingese, a Japanese Chin, or one of the Tibetan breeds described in these pages will remind you, dear reader, of the lion-dogs' long and eventful history. And please keep in mind that in spite of their small size they greatly appreciate being treated with the respect due the dogs of Fo.

POSTSCRIPT

Descendant of a demon sky-dog and a savage lion tamed and domesticated by the Buddha, the dog-lion has watched over sacred mountains, graveyards, temples, altars, thrones, homes, and government buildings in many Buddhist countries down through the centuries. The ribbon or cord that the Buddhist creature often holds in his mouth is attached to the ball, or jewel, as the Enlightened One's teaching is called by Buddhists. The ribbon may symbolize the bond which Buddhists believe joins beings of all times, countries, religions, and even species.

Whether woven in wool, worked in wood, or carved in precious jade, all materials of great significance in three different

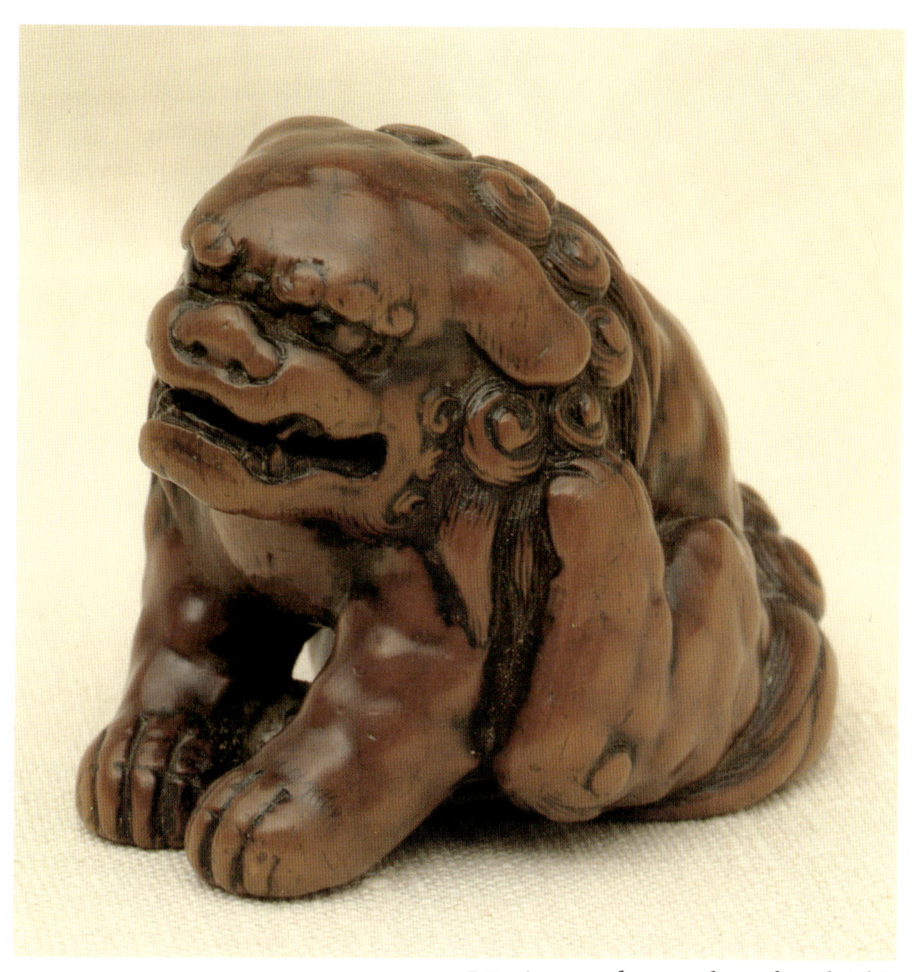

56. A wood netsuke of a shishi.

cultures, the Buddha-dog has insinuated himself into intimate human situations. From the wool rug with which the Tibetan nomad covered himself on cold nights, to the toggle which secured containers for pipes and medicines to the obi of the Japanese merchant, to the jade ornament for the Chinese scholar's desk, the guardian dog-lion's presence has been ubiquitous in domestic as well as official and religious settings. Scholars may never agree on the sources or significance of his periwinkle curls, ball, ribbons, and great owl eyes. However, beyond dispute is the association of the dog of Fo with the Buddha and his ethic of compassion for all beings, some of whom have been extensively and willfully abused by humankind.

In Asia there have been many other popular beasts of fable: the dragon, the unicorn, the phoenix, and the baku, all of whom strike responsive chords in the human psyche. However, not even the supremely favored dragon, imposing symbol of emperors, was accompanied by an alter ego, a flesh-and-blood incarnation. It is the small, beguiling flesh-and-blood manifestations of the dog-lion that have become particularly well known and cherished by so many in the modern West.

In conclusion, I would like to draw the reader's attention to the dynamic spirit-lions painted each morning by the Japanese painter and printmaker Hokusai (1760–1849). Before starting

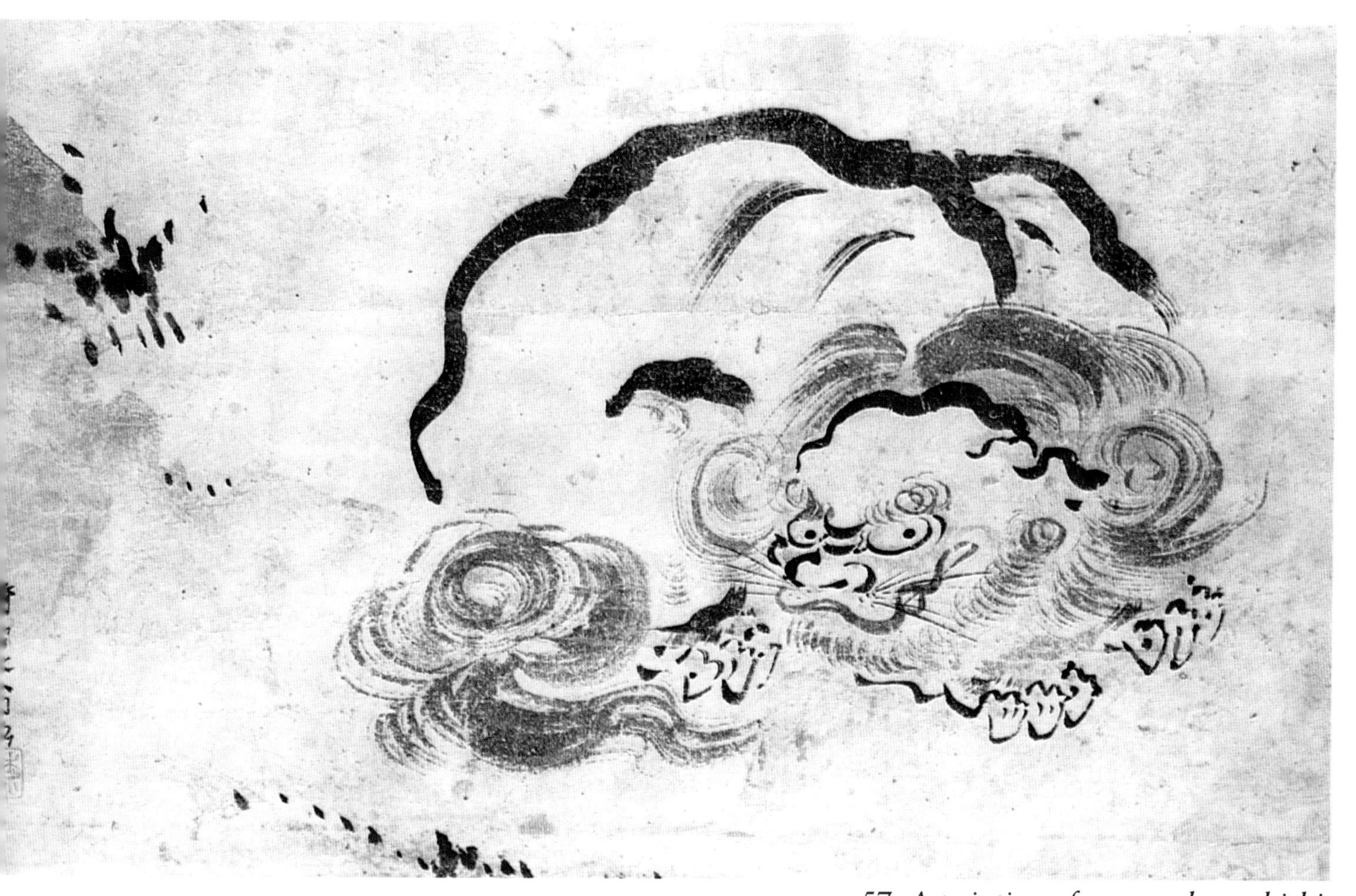

57. A painting of a recumbent shishi.

on his work of the day, the master vigorously created with his brush a great number of shishi. Thus he drove all distractions and evil spirits from his mind and heart, leaving himself in what Zen Buddhists call *mushin,* the state of perfect awareness and receptivity to the creative muse.

COMMENTARIES
ON THE PLATES

1. This fierce guardian dog-lion is from the Lara-Jonggrang temple in Central Java, Indonesia. Carved, appropriately, from volcanic rock, he has a thick neck and prominent owllike eyes. The figure is from the late ninth or early tenth century. Height 54 cm (about 21¼ in.), width 30 cm (about 11¾ in.), length 40 cm (about 15¾ in.). Courtesy, Museum of Fine Arts, Boston; gift of John Goelet, Constance B. and Carroll L. Cartwright. By exchange.

2. From Okinawa comes this modern Japanese *mingei* (folk art) representation of a shishi. The earthenware shishi is actually a bell, since his hollow stomach contains a metal ball. Height 3¼ in., length 3½ in. Courtesy of a private collector. Photo by Dean Powell.

3. The historic château of Fontainebleau, in France, more than eight centuries old, is home to an extraordinary collection of sculpted Greek and Roman deities, as well as classical nymphs and cupids. In the sixteenth century King Francis I, impressed by the antiquity of Egyptian monuments, installed sandstone sculptures of Isis and Osiris at the entrance of the passageway leading from his garden into the great court. In the nineteenth century, under Emperor Napoleon III, a Chinese museum with objects from the summer palace in Beijing and a Chinese room for the empress were added to this remarkable château. The female stone guardian depicted here surveys one of the courtyards and the misty French landscape beyond. She supports a long-legged, almost reptilian offspring. Photo by John Roland Hill.

4. A Chinese quartz Fu dog and offspring frolic around a large ball with incised decorations. A ribbon falls in folds from the mother's left forepaw around the ball and is caught up and thrown into the air by her right hind leg. The baby, perched on the ball, happily watches his mother's spirited performance. The wooden base simulates a cloud. Height 4½ in. Courtesy of a private collector. Photo by Dean Powell.

5. A favored decoration for Chinese earthenware and china, the Fo dogs ornamenting the four sides of this porcelain tea caddy display splendid vitality as they play with their balls, ribbons, and tassels. Fo dogs are often depicted on porcelain plates, bowls, vases, and garden seats. China candlesticks, incense burners, vase handles, and finials are frequently in the form of dogs of Fo seated, recumbent, or rampant. Height 7½ in. Courtesy of a private collector. Photo by Dean Powell.

6. Black or solid gold (red) Shih Tzu are more unusual than those with mixed, or parti-colored, coats. In China a gold dog was known as a "sun dog." The black Shih Tzu depicted here is only eight inches at the withers, an inch shorter than required by the American Kennel Club standard. Both dogs in this painting are partially trimmed. Shih Tzu are exhibited in shows with long trailing coats and topknots. Oil portrait by Robert Johnson.

7. The modern show-type Pekingese has short, bowed forelegs and, like the Tibetan Spaniel and the Japanese Chin, has a long, or "hare," foot. He is heavy-chested and has a large, thick ruff. The Peke bred for today's show ring also has wrinkles on his broad muzzle. The ancestors of the Shih Tzu more closely resembled the Japanese Chin of today. Oil portrait by Robert Johnson.

8. A stylish little dog, the Japanese Chin is probably the Pekingese as he originally was when sent from China to Japan in the seventh century A.D. Like the Pug, he has long, straight legs. He resembles the Pekingese, both modern and ancient, and has large eyes, a broad skull, and a flat face. The American Kennel Club maintains two size categories for the Chin: over seven and under seven pounds. He may be black and white, lemon and white, or red and white. Oil portrait by Robert Johnson.

9. In Tibet the Lhasa Apso is sometimes known as "the bark lion sentinel dog"; his special task is to alert giant Tibetan Mastiffs, the outdoor dogs, when intruders are about. The Lhasa, an indoor companion dog, and one of the ancestors of the Shih Tzu, differs from the usually smaller Shih Tzu mainly in his narrower skull, longer nose, and smaller eyes. However, hid-

den as he is beneath a long, sweeping coat, he may be difficult to distinguish from the Shih Tzu. Oil portrait by Robert Johnson.

10. A nineteenth-century Japanese wood netsuke, this mother shishi surveys her baby as he clambers onto her back. Her eyes are inlaid in brass, and there is some red staining. The netsuke is signed Minko. Height 1 in. Courtesy of a private collector. Photo by Dean Powell.

11, 12. Presently guarding a driveway in Marion, Massachusetts, are this pair of early-nineteenth-century stone dog-lions from China. Of particular interest are their expressions. The mouth of the male is open as he repeats the first half of the sacred mantric syllable *aum,* while his partner's mouth is closed in the concluding *mmm.* Height 32 in., width 27 in. Courtesy of Janice Mendes. Photos by Dean Powell.

13. This compact Indian lion, with his wide face, prominent eyes, and stylized curls, bears a strong resemblance to the dog-lions of China. The stone Gupta sculpture dates from the fifth or sixth century A.D. Height 19¾ in. Courtesy, Museum of Fine Arts, Boston; bequest of Charles Ames Cummings.

14, 15. From China come this splendidly caparisoned pair of gilt and turquoise Fo lions. According to Corneille Jest, in Tibet "la couleur turquoise, dont on pare par example la lionne gardienne, est la couleur noble par excellence." Both male and female have flower-covered red collars, and on their broad chests are golden lion's-head crests from which hang long tassels affixed with rings. Gilded tassels are attached to each side of the collar, and down the center of each dog-lion's back is an enormous bow with a gilded rosette in its center. The cloissonné pair are seated on tablelike stands with altar cloth–shaped coverings that fold down over the sides. The female places her large paw over her offspring's stomach. He lies on his back staring up into his mother's face. The sire's paw rests on a red and gold ball from which sinuously flows a gold ribbon (made from a separate piece of metal) that falls from the ball and over the side of the Fo lion's seat. Height 30 in., length 21 in. Courtesy of a private collector. Photos by Stephen B. Leek.

16, 17. At the mountain temple Eihei-ji, in Japan's Fukui Prefecture, four grinning white koma-inu, or "Korean dogs," on rectangular plinths guard the altar of the Hatto, or teaching hall. These straight-legged Korean dogs have snail-curls on the tops of their heads and details picked out with gilding and paint. They have small doglike teeth, and humorous expressions. Photos by J. Tada Studio.

18. This "double *oban*" print, actually two prints joined, by the woodblock artist Hiroshige (1797–1858) depicts a mother shishi surveying her offspring as he appears to be successfully completing his ascent of a steep cliff. He thus proves his worthiness to serve the Buddha. The parent shishi's expression is one of maternal satisfaction as she peers down at her offspring's travails. Courtesy of a private collector. Photo by Dean Powell.

19, 20. In the late nineteenth and early twentieth centuries considerable detail was added to the design of balls and harnesses, as well as to the faces of many Chinese dog-lions. Offspring proliferated, and a parent creature with multiple young under a forepaw was occasionally called the grandfather Fo; the young ones symbolize filial piety. This very large stone pair, each figure weighing 3,500 pounds, have bald heads and snaillike curls on the chin and down the center of the back; their legs and feet have an almost dragonlike appearance. There is elaborate detail on external balls and ribbons. One of the young is perched on his own small ball, indicating that he is of the desirable male sex. The smooth ball in the mouth of each figure symbolizes the Dharma, or Buddhist teaching. These remarkable creatures now have their own handsome atrium in the Peabody Museum of Salem, Massachusetts. Height 64 in., width 30 in., length 50 in. Courtesy of the Peabody Museum of Salem. Photos by Mark Sexton.

21. Manjusri, the bodhisattva of wisdom, is revered by the adherents of the Zen sect of Buddhism. This tiny modern Japanese wood carving depicts Manjusri seated on his lotus throne, which is supported by his faithful shishi. A small section of Manjusri's scepter is missing. Height ⅝ in., length ½ in. Courtesy of a private collector. Photo by Dean Powell.

22, 23. This nephrite group of a mother Fu dog and her two offspring is attributed to the Ming dynasty. One of the babies plays with a brocade ball, while the other grasps the trailing end of a ribbon which terminates in a large bow on the mother's underside. The mother holds the other end of the ribbon in her mouth. Height 4⅜ in., length 6⅜ in. Courtesy of a private collector. Photos by Dean Powell.

24. In this pair of seated nephrite Fu dogs with wide-open mouths, the mother's protective paw partly covers the head of her plaintively open-

mouthed baby, while the sire's paw is firmly wrapped over the top of his brocade ball. Each parent creature wears a thick collar with a bell and has the character yu incised on the forehead. Here yu indicates an imperial pair. Height 9½ in., length at base 7 in. Courtesy of a private collector. Photo by Dean Powell.

25. From the seventeenth century comes this recumbent one-horned Fu dog or bixie. A lingzhi, or sacred fungus, trails from his mouth; the fungus and its leafy vines encircle the little creature's head and are draped over his back and around his feet. His partially curled, chocolate-colored tail is carried gracefully over his back in true lion-dog fashion. During the Ming dynasty small nephrite animals like this were prized as ornaments for a scholar's writing table. Height 2¼ in., length 4¼ in. Courtesy of a private collector. Photo by Dean Powell.

26. This nephrite toggle of a mother Fu dog holding her offspring under a forepaw (perforated to allow a cord to run from the base to the tail of the figure) is attributed to the Tang dynasty. The cub's head is turned back as if he were inspecting his mother's paw. The stone is a very pale yellow with russet splashes on the mane and haunches of the mother. In front of the baby is a brocaded ball tied with a long ribbon which the mother holds in her mouth. Loose ribbons from the other side of the ball fall under the two figures. Height 1⅝ in., length 1¼ in. Courtesy of a private collector. Photo by Dean Powell.

27. From the sixteenth century comes this stoneware dog-lion with turquoise mane, tail, and feathering. Draped through his open jaws is a grace-

ful turquoise ribbon, and he wears a simple turquoise collar with a small bell. He gazes wistfully and perhaps expectantly heavenward. Height 9¾ in. Courtesy, Museum of Fine Arts, Boston; gift of Mrs. F. G. Macomber.

28. Believed to date from the seventeenth century, this nephrite bixie is curled up like a cat. His head and single horn are seen in profile. Height 1¾ in., length 2 in. Courtesy of a private collector. Photo by Stephen B. Leek.

29. In the form of an archaic Chinese incense burner, this wood shishi stands with his feet together and his head raised. His open mouth contains a loose ball symbolizing the Buddhist teaching. The netsuke dates from the mid-nineteenth century. Height 1⅜ in. Courtesy of a private collector. Photo by Dean Powell.

30. This ebullient seventeenth-century shishi stands on his forepaws and flings his hind legs in the air. The figure is of Arita ware. Height 11¾ in. Courtesy of a private collector. Photo courtesy of Sotheby's.

31. Decorated with a gold and silver design of a frog jumping in a field of wild flowers, this four-tier inro was made in the nineteenth century. The attached netsuke is a wood shishi perched on a *mokugyo,* a hollow wooden drum used in Buddhist ceremonies. Length of inro 3¼ in. Courtesy of a private collector. Photo by Dean Powell.

32. This mid-nineteenth-century wood netsuke shows a shishi being born from an egg: the baby shishi's head and front paws are emerging from the

broken shell. Height 1½ in. Courtesy of a private collector. Photo by Dean Powell.

33. This florally decorated wood netsuke from the nineteenth century is in the form of a ball enclosing an intricately carved standing shishi, who can be viewed through three round openings. A much smaller himotoshi, or hole for a cord, gives a fourth view of the shishi. Height 1½ in. Courtesy of a private collector. Photo by Dean Powell.

34. This spirited wood shishi from the Edo period was probably one of a series of ornaments which once surmounted the entrance of a Buddhist temple. Like the Arita-ware shishi in plate 30, he is unfettered and joyful. Height 11¼ in. Courtesy of a private collector. Photo by Richard Cheek.

35. These shishi, one recumbent and one standing on his hind legs waving his forepaws, have large, elaborate tails which meet to form the himotoshi. The heads of the shishi are covered with knobby whorls. This wood netsuke was carved by Sadanobu in the nineteenth century. Height 1½ in. Courtesy of a private collector. Photo by Dean Powell.

36. Curled into a sphere, this boxwood shishi has a wide-open mouth containing a ball, symbol of the Buddhist Dharma. The netsuke was carved in the early nineteenth century. Height 1⅛ in. Courtesy of a private collector. Photo by Dean Powell.

37. Signed by Shuraku, this wood netsuke dates from the mid-nineteenth century. A boy wearing a large shishi mask of the kind used in the lion

dance grasps a drum between his legs and holds a pair of drumsticks in his hands. The boy's head can be seen within the mask; his eyes and nose are just visible between the shishi's teeth. Height 1¼ in. Courtesy of a private collector. Photo by Dean Powell.

38. An exceptional netsuke from the late eighteenth century, this wood baku stands with outstretched legs, his trunk lowered to a hind paw, his curly tail erect over his back. He gives every indication of being capable of vigorous action to banish nightmares. Height 2⅛ in. Courtesy of a private collector. Photo by Bruce Peterson.

39. A large wood netsuke from the late eighteenth century, this shishi is seated, his head lowered as he grasps a peony in his mouth. The shishi, king of the beasts, appropriately amuses himself with the king of the flowers, as the peony is called in Japan. Height 2⅛ in. Courtesy of a private collector. Photo by Dean Powell.

40. This small Lhasa Apso, or "hairy one," was bred by Tibetans in Nepal. According to Corneille Jest, both large and small varieties of the Lhasa originated in central Tibet, where the altitude is twelve thousand to sixteen thousand feet. The small white dog in this photo bears the name Nyinjé (Beautiful). He is held by Lama Gyurmé Trakpa. Photo courtesy of Harold Talbott.

41. Tibetan Terriers, the largest of the hairy Tibetan dogs, are called by the Tibetans "the little people." A dog's height may be fourteen to sixteen inches, and he may weigh between eighteen and thirty pounds. The Tibetan

Terrier is not a real terrier, and he does not have a terrier disposition. He was not trained to pursue small animals underground. ("Terrier" is derived from the French *terre,* "earth.") In old Tibet he was a companion dog and was known as "the luck bringer." He may be any color or combination of colors and is rugged and healthy, comfortable in either very cold or hot climates. Oil portrait by Robert Johnson.

42. Bred in the villages of Tibet, the Tibetan Spaniel, like other Tibetan breeds, appears in all colors and mixtures of colors. The longer-muzzled types of Tibetan dogs were found west of the Tibetan capital of Lhasa, so there was less likely to be an admixture of genes from flat-faced Chinese dogs. According to the official American Kennel Club book, *The Complete Dog Book,* "it is not surprising to find other Tibetan breeds occasionally producing Tibetan Spaniel–type puppies." Oil portrait by Robert Johnson.

43. From *Himmelsstier und Gletscherlöwe,* by Matthias Hermanns, comes the following quotation: "The mountain peak reaches up toward heaven to rival the mountain glacier. There the white lion [kang seng] strides about in all his exuberance, showing off his majestic turquoise mane" (my translation). The kang seng is generally believed to have turquoise claws and a turquoise mane, tail, and feathering on the backs of his legs. However, modern weavers in India and Nepal often prefer green or blue yarns, as in the case of this rug. 42 in. x 30 in. Courtesy of a private collector. Photo by Stephen B. Leek.

44, 45. This nineteenth-century Tibetan rug from Nepal has a velvet border and a flowered silk backing. The sedate Chinese-inspired dog-lion with his ball, in the center, is of faded turquoise with white ears, paws, and tail. The hundred-year-old rug has earth-tone colors softened by time and use. 60 in. x 30½ in. including velvet border. Courtesy of a private collector. Photo by Dean Powell.

46, 47. Woven in unusual colors, this twentieth-century Tibetan rug depicts an important Buddhist theme. The central figure is the face of a pre-Buddhist sea monster called the *makara* in Sanskrit, the *ch'u-srin* in Tibetan. Before his transformation by the Buddhist teaching, this monster pleased himself by killing and eating any living creatures, including human beings, who had the misfortune to inhabit or to fall into a body of water. Converted to Buddhism, the bloodthirsty demon became a significant symbol of spiritual transformation. His curious visage is found on the corners of Tibetan temple roofs and on the handles of temple doors. On this rug the makara is surrounded by a snow-lion (kang seng), a tiger, a dragon, and an eagle, symbols of power, energy, strength, and courage inspired by the spirit of the Buddha. In the four corners of the rug are stylized waves, and the makara is flanked by clouds. 72 in. x 36 in. Courtesy of a private collector. Photo by Dean Powell.

48. This dog-lion, a Cambodian box of chased silver, appears overfed and humorous. Height 3 in., length 4 in. Courtesy of a private collector. Photo by Dean Powell.

49. Wearing a benign and cheerful expression, this particularly canine dog-lion is in the form of a Chinese silver incense holder (the back contains an opening for powdered incense). His collar, with its tassel and bells, is of the

sort worn by pampered pets at the Manchu court. The beads that dangle from his feet, as well as those from which he is suspended, are modern additions. Height 3½ in., length 2¾ in. Courtesy of a private collector. Photo by Dean Powell.

50, 51. This Chinese statue of Guanyin (Avalokitesvara in Sanskrit), the bodhisattva of compassion, protector of all creatures whether two- or four-legged, is guarded by four Indian-style dog-lions. The two in front appear to be on guard, while the pair in the rear are relaxed, as if off duty. The statue, dating from around A.D. 580, is of polychrome stone. Height 2.49 cm (about 1 in.). Courtesy, Museum of Fine Arts, Boston; Asiatic Curators Fund.

52. In the twelve Longmen cave-temples of Henan Province, central China, spectacular Buddhist sculptures were created and enshrined between 493 and 674. In 672 or 673 a colossal image of Vairocana Buddha (thirty-five feet high, on a pedestal fifteen feet high) was made for this remarkable setting. The Buddhist guardian lion pictured here is also from the late seventh century. He holds a braided cord in his mouth and has a bell around his neck. This limestone figure, one of a pair, once stood in the antechamber to the Cave of Ten Thousand Buddhas. Height 48 in. Courtesy, Museum of Fine Arts, Boston; Rebecca R. Joslin Fund.

53. Seated on a tablelike base, this white stone mother Fo dog with offspring protected the entrance to an elegant store in Palm Beach, Florida, until one morning her mate disappeared from his place. Mother with baby and missing mate were replaced by a similar couple about four times the

size and weight of the original pair. Height 24 in., length 10 in. Courtesy of a private collector. Photo by Stephen B. Leek.

54, 55. This curious Chinese wood tile depicts an altar with flowers and an incense burner. The altar is flanked by smaller ornamental tables bearing objects that must have been cherished in a well-to-do middle-class Chinese household around the turn of the twentieth century, including a phonograph with a morning glory–shaped speaker. Under the altar a large Fo dog appears to have made a descent, bringing with him a large decorated ball attached to cords which the creature grasps in his mouth and draws after him. Height 6½ in., width 13 in. Courtesy of a private collector. Photos by Dean Powell.

56. From the late eighteenth or early nineteenth century, this wood-netsuke shishi holds in his open mouth three small loose balls, symbolizing the Buddha, his teaching, and his community. The carving was made by Chikuyo-sai Tomochika. Height 5.3 cm (about 2 in.). Courtesy of a private collector. Photo by Dean Powell.

57. This recumbent shishi was painted by a Japanese artist of the Kano school. Though at rest, the creature conveys an impression of intense watchfulness and latent energy. Courtesy of a private collector. Photo by Dean Powell.

NOTES

Reliable sources on the multifaceted subject of the dog-lion/lion-dog are few and not readily accessible. Rumer Godden's charming book on the Pekingese, *The Butterfly Lions,* is based largely on V. W. F. Collier's *Dogs of China and Japan in Nature and Art.* According to Miss Godden, Mr. Collier lived in China, spoke Chinese, and acquired his knowledge from primary sources. I have found his book to be of invaluable assistance.

Books on pure-bred dogs, including Miss Godden's, emphasize the uniqueness of a particular breed. I have taken another approach and have emphasized the relationship of Chinese, Japanese, and Tibetan lion-dogs. This relationship is suggested by H. Epstein in his *Domestic Animals of China* and by Kim Dennis-Bryan and Juliet Clutton-Brock in their *Dogs of the Last Hundred Years at the British Museum (Natural History).*

Chapter six includes quotations from "Huei Chao's Pilgrimage

Through Northwest India and Central Asia (circa A.D. 726)," my translation of the German translation of an extract of Huei Chao's journal. The German translation was made by Walter Fuchs in Beijing in 1938, and I put this into English nearly forty years ago. The original document is in the Bibliothèque Nationale, in Paris.

The reference notes to the introduction and each chapter follow an abbreviated style. Complete information on all the works cited in the notes will be found in the bibliography.

INTRODUCTION: CELESTIAL DOGS, DOG-LIONS, AND LION-DOGS

Pp. 11–12. For descriptions of celestial dogs, see Peter Lum, *Fabulous Beasts,* pp. 85–86; Rumer Godden, *The Butterfly Lions,* p. 21.

P. 12. "le génie de la race." T. Volker, *The Animal in Far Eastern Art,* p. 6.

CHAPTER ONE: FLESH-AND-FUR LION-DOGS

P. 30. "In Ssechuan . . . early warning of trouble outside." V. W. F. Collier, *Dogs of China and Japan in Nature and Art,* p. 133.

P. 31. "dogges curled and rough . . . of face nor of body." Quoted in ibid., p. 145.

P. 34. "These beasts . . . bred in their homes." Quoted in ibid., p. 134.

CHAPTER TWO: LIONS AND DOG-LIONS

P. 63. "breathes . . . and inspirits them." J. L. Schrader, "A Medieval Bestiary," p. 12.

P. 63. "the unborn, the unbecome, the unmade." Udana VIII, quoted in Sarvepalli Radhakrishnan and Charles A. Moore, eds., *A Source Book in Indian Philosophy,* p. 636.

CHAPTER THREE: THE DOG OF FO AND THE JADE MYSTIQUE OF CHINA

In writing this chapter I consulted a Chinese work, *Arts and Crafts: Jade*, volume 9 of *Great Treasury of Chinese Fine Arts*. Lei Kai kindly made translations of excerpts available to me.

P. 70. "is formed . . . the surface of the earth"; "Nephrite . . . closer to the earth's surface." Richard Gump, *Jade: Stone of Heaven*, p. 31.

P. 71. "Smash two diamonds . . . remain intact." Ibid., p. 24.

P. 71. "most completely Chinese of all materials." Ibid., p. 26.

P. 74. "a place accorded . . . blessings in return." Ibid., p. 58.

P. 76. "Do not wish to be . . . common like stone." Ibid., p. 108.

P. 80. "The Eastern dragon . . . only to vanish." Okakura Kakuzo, *The Awakening of Japan*, pp. 77–78.

P. 87. "the propitious air . . . is always condensing into jade." Gump, *Jade*, p. 69.

CHAPTER FOUR: THE SHISHI AND THE ART OF THE JAPANESE NETSUKE

P. 98. For a discussion of aji, see Barbra T. Okada, *Netsuke: Masterpieces from the Metropolitan Museum of Art*, p. 11.

Pp. 99–100. "When ninth century esoteric Buddhist sculptors . . . as natural a form as possible." Elizabeth ten Grotenhuis, "Japanese Buddhism and Its Influence on the Visual Arts," pp. 11–12.

P. 112. "The sacred one-horned suisei . . . reflection in its eyes." Paul Moss, *Japanese Netsuke: Serious Art*.

CHAPTER FIVE: LION-DOGS, SNOW-LIONS, AND THE ARTS OF TIBET

I am grateful to Harold Talbott and to Lama Khenpo Palden Sherab for their help and their answers to my questions about the snow-lion of Tibet.

P. 114. "la consommation de viande est occasionelle." Corneille Jest, *La Turquoise de Vie: Un pèlerinage tibétain.*

P. 116. The information on religious names for dogs is from Robert Ekvall, "Role of the Dog in Tibetan Nomadic Society," pp. 164–65.

P. 122. "If the snow-lion . . . it becomes a dog." Lama Khenpo Palden Sherab.

P. 126. "The fair Mount Chimbu . . . soaring into the sky." David Snellgrove, *Buddhist Himalaya,* p. 153; quoted in Pratapaditya Pal, *The Art of Tibet,* p. 38.

P. 128. "a house of carpets." Dianak Myers, *Temple, Household, Horseback: Rugs of the Tibetan Plateau,* p. 53.

Pp. 129–30. The information on the washing of fleece is from William C. C. Hu and Virginia Dulany Hyman, *Carpets of China and Its Border Regions,* p. 135.

CHAPTER SIX: DOGS, OTHER NON-HUMAN BEINGS, AND BUDDHISM

P. 134. "I, Ahura Mazda . . . and the house dog." *Zend Avesta,* vol. 4 of *Sacred Books of the East,* ed. Max Müller, p. 160; quoted in V. W. F. Collier, *Dogs of China and Japan in Nature and Art,* p. 13.

P. 135. "If the bones . . . this is a sin." Ibid.

P. 139. "What is an infant . . . in the shape of a man?" Keith Thomas, *Man and the Natural World: A History of the Modern Sensibility,* p. 43.

P. 140. The information on the Gutenberg Bible is from Curt F. Buhler, *The Fifteenth Century Book,* p. 42; quoted in Thomas, *Man and the Natural World,* p. 25 n.

P. 142. "there was no civilized land 'where . . . so many varieties of it.'" Thomas, *Man and the Natural World,* p. 108.

P. 143. "The wise look upon . . . a svapaka as alike." *Sacred Books of the East,* vol. 8, p. 65; quoted in Collier, *Dogs of China and Japan,* p. 37.

Pp. 144–46. "Thus Mahamati . . . refrain from eating meat"; "Mahamati, there is . . . I do not permit." Daisetz T. Suzuki, trans., *The Lankavatara Sutra: A Mahayana Text,* pp. 212, 214, 218, 219.

P. 147. "eat the fruit of his deeds." Vincent Smith, ed., *The Edicts of Asoka,* p. xiii.

P. 147. "Here . . . shall not be slaughtered." Ibid., p. 7.

P. 148. "Everywhere has . . . man and beast." Ibid., pp. 7–8.

P. 148. "Father and mother . . . must be practised." Ibid., p. 5.

Pp. 150–52. All quotations from Huei Chao's journal are from my translation of Walter Fuchs, trans., "Huei Chao: Pilgerreise durch Nordwestindien und Zentralasien um 726."

P. 154. "Out of necessity . . . of all beings." Tetsuya Inoue, "Dignity of Life," in *Human Dignity and Medicine,* ed. J. Bernard, K. Kajikawa, and N. Fujiki, p. 11.

P. 154. The Japanese memorial service for whales is described in Philip Kapleau, *To Cherish All Life: A Buddhist Case for Becoming Vegetarian,* p. 47.

P. 155. The funeral in Sri Lanka is described in the *Boston Globe,* July 31, 1988.

POSTSCRIPT

Pp. 162–64. The information on the shishi paintings of Hokusai is from T. Volker, *The Animal in Far Eastern Art,* p. 111.

BIBLIOGRAPHY

Ahir, D. C. *Buddhist Shrines in India*. B. R. Publishing Corp., 1986.

American Kennel Club. *The Complete Dog Book*. Howell Book House, 1986.

Arakawa, Hirokazu. *The Gō Collection of Netsuke: Tokyo National Museum*. Kodansha International, 1983.

Baten, Lea. *Japanese Animal Art—Antique & Contemporary*. Shufuno-tomo, 1989.

Burn, Andrew. *The World of Hesiod*. Ayer, 1966.

Bushell, Raymond. *Netsuke Familiar and Unfamiliar*. Weatherhill, 1975.

Carson, Gerald. *Men, Beasts and Gods*. Scribners, 1972.

Collier, V. W. F. *Dogs of China and Japan in Nature and Art*. Frederick A. Stokes, 1921.

Craven, Roy C. *Indian Art*. Thames and Hudson, 1976.

Dadds, Audrey. *The Shih Tzu.* Howell Book House, 1974.

Davey, Neil K. *Netsuke: A Comprehensive Study Based on the M. T. Hindson Collection.* Sotheby Park Bernet, 1974.

Dennis-Bryan, Kim, and Juliet Clutton-Brock. *Dogs of the Last Hundred Years at the British Museum (Natural History).* British Museum, 1988.

Dixe, Annie Coath. *The Lion-Dog of Peking.* Peter Davies, 1931.

Easton, D. Allan, and Joan McDonald Brearley. *This Is the Shih Tzu.* TFH Publications, n.d.

Edwards, Lisa A., and Margie M. Krebs. *Netsuke: The Collection of the Peabody Museum of Salem.* Peabody Museum of Salem, 1980.

Ekvall, Robert. "Role of the Dog in Tibetan Nomadic Society." *Central Asiatic Journal,* vol. 8 (September 1963).

Epstein, H. *Domestic Animals of China.* Commonwealth Agricultural Bureau, 1969.

Ferrante, Jon. *Shih Tzu Heritage.* Denlinger's Publishers, 1989.

Fuchs, Walter, trans. "Huei Chao: Pilgerreise durch Nordwestindien und Zentralasien um 726." *Sitzungberichte der preussischen Akademie,* 1938.

Gans-Ruedin, E. *Chinese Carpets.* Kodansha International, 1981.

Godden, Rumer. *The Butterfly Lions.* Viking, 1977.

Gump, Richard. *Jade: Stone of Heaven.* Doubleday, 1962.

Hansford, S. Howard. *Chinese Jade Carving.* Lund, Humphries, 1950.

Harris, Victor. *Netsuke.* British Museum, 1987.

Hartman-Goldsmith, Joan. *Chinese Jade.* Oxford University Press, 1986.

Herbet, Norman, and Carolyn Herbet. *The Complete Lhasa Apso.* Howell Book House, 1986.

Hermanns, Matthias. *Himmelsstier und Gletscherlöwe*. Eric Roth–Verlag, 1955.

Hu, William C. C., and Virginia Dulany Hyman. *Carpets of China and Its Border Regions*. Ars Ceramica, 1982.

Inoue, Tetsuya. "Dignity of Life." In *Human Dignity and Medicine*, ed. J. Bernard, K. Kajikawa, and N. Fujiki. Elsevier Science Publishers, 1988.

Jest, Corneille. *La Turquoise de Vie: Un pèlerinage tibétain*. Éditions A. M. Métailié, 1985.

Kapleau, Philip. *To Cherish All Life: A Buddhist Case for Becoming Vegetarian*. Harper and Row, 1982.

Kozloff, Arielle P., ed. *Animals in Ancient Art from the Leo Mildenberg Collection*. Cleveland Museum of Art, 1982.

Lum, Peter. *Fabulous Beasts*. Thames and Hudson, n.d.

Majuparia, Trilok Chandra. *Sacred and Symbolic Animals of Nepal*. Sahayogi Press, 1977.

Moss, Paul. *Japanese Netsuke: Serious Art*. Sydney L. Moss, 1989.

Myers, Dianak. *Temple, Household, Horseback: Rugs of the Tibetan Plateau*. Textile Museum, 1984.

O'Brien, M. L. *Netsuke: A Guide for Collectors*. Charles E. Tuttle, 1980.

Okada, Barbra T. *Netsuke: Masterpieces from the Metropolitan Museum of Art*. Harry N. Abrams, 1982.

———. "Netsuke: The Small Sculptures of Japan." *Metropolitan Museum of Art Bulletin* (Fall 1980).

———, with Mary G. Neill. *Real and Imaginary Beings: The Netsuke Collection of Joseph and Edith Kurstin*. Yale University Art Gallery, 1980.

Okakura Kakuzo. *The Awakening of Japan*. Century, 1904.

Pal, Pratapaditya. *The Art of Tibet*. Asia Society, 1969.

Radhakrishnan, Sarvepalli, and Charles A. Moore, eds. *A Source Book in Indian Philosophy*. Princeton University Press, 1957.

Rosenfield, John, and Elizabeth ten Grotenhuis. *Journey of the Three Jewels: Japanese Buddhist Paintings from Western Collections*. Asia Society, 1979.

Schrader, J. L. "A Medieval Bestiary." *Metropolitan Museum of Art Bulletin* (Summer 1986).

Seattle Art Museum. *In Pursuit of the Dragon*. Seattle Art Museum, 1988.

Sickman, Laurence, and Alexander Soper. *The Art and Architecture of China*. Penguin, 1956.

Smith, Vincent, ed. *The Edicts of Asoka*. Essex House Press, 1909.

Suzuki, Daisetz T., trans. *The Lankavatara Sutra: A Mahayana Text*. Reprint. Routledge and Kegan Paul, 1968.

ten Grotenhuis, Elizabeth. "Japanese Buddhism and Its Influence on the Visual Arts." Unpublished manuscript.

Thomas, Keith. *Man and the Natural World: A History of the Modern Sensibility*. Pantheon, 1983.

Tucci, Guiseppe. *Tibet: Land of Snows*. Stein and Day, 1967.

Volker, T. *The Animal in Far Eastern Art*. E. J. Brill, 1950.

Watson, William. *Art of Dynastic China*. Harry N. Abrams, 1983.

Watt, James C. Y. *Chinese Jades from Han to Ch'ing*. Asia Society, 1980.

Weisbrod, Michael B. *Dragons, Monsters and Auspicious Beasts*. Michael B. Weisbrod, 1988.

Williams, C. A. S. *Outlines of Chinese Symbolism & Art Motives*. 3d rev. ed. Dover, 1976.

Yang Boda, ed. *Arts and Crafts: Jade*. Vol. 9 of *Great Treasury of Chinese Fine Arts*. Cultural Objects Publishing House, 1986.

Yang Hanchen et al. *Xinjiang's Gems and Jades*. Xinjiang People's Publishing House, 1986.
Zimmer, Heinrich. *Myths and Symbols in Indian Art and Civilization*. Harper, 1962.

FOR CHILDREN

Godden, Rumer. *Fu-Dog*. Viking, 1990.
Harris, Rosemary. *The Little Dog of Fo*. Faber and Faber, 1976.

INDEX